Trapped at Pearl Harbor

TRAPPED AT

PEARL HARBOR

Escape from Battleship Oklahoma

STEPHEN BOWER YOUNG

NORTH RIVER PRESS
Croton-on-Hudson, New York
and
NAVAL INSTITUTE PRESS
Annapolis, Maryland

First published in the United States of America by
Naval Institute Press, Annapolis, Maryland, and North
River Press, Croton-on-Hudson, New York.

Library of Congress Cataloging-in-Publication Data

Young, Stephen Bower.
Trapped at Pearl Harbor : escape from Battleship
Oklahoma / Stephen Bower Young.
p.   cm.
Includes index.
ISBN 1-55750-975-1
1. Young, Stephen Bower. 2. *Oklahoma* (Battleship)
3. World War, 1939–1945—Personal narratives,
American. 4. Pearl Harbor (Hawaii), Attack on, 1941.
5. United States. Navy—Gunners—Biography.
6. Seamen—United States—Biography. I. Title.
D774.04Y68   1991
940.54'26—dc20
[B]   90-28606

Printed in the United States of America on
acid-free paper ∞

2   4   6   8   9   7   5   3

To the sailors and marines who lost their lives
on board the ships in Pearl Harbor,
Territory of Hawaii, on 7 December 1941,
and in particular those men of the battleship
Oklahoma's 4th deck division
and the crew of no. 4 gun turret

When I have fears that I may cease to be
    Before my pen has gleaned my teeming brain,
Before high-pil'ed books, in charact'ry,
    Hold like rich garners the full-ripened grain;
When I behold, upon the night's starred face,
    Huge cloudy symbols of a high romance,
And think that I may never live to trace
    Their shadows, with the magic hand of chance;
And when I feel, fair creature of an hour,
    That I shall never look upon thee more,
Never have relish in the faery power
    Of unreflecting love! — then on the shore
Of the wide world I stand alone, and think
    Till Love and Fame to nothingness do sink.

JOHN KEATS

Contents

Preface

This account is a true and faithful report on the lives of a few dozen sailors, members of the 14-inch gun crew of the battleship *Oklahoma*'s turret no. 4, and some others, mostly young, who were caught up in the swirl of a world at war on a sunny Sunday morning in Hawaii, 7 December 1941. The assault took place when a daring Japanese carrier force invaded the friendly waters of the islands and in a surprise attack smashed the mighty U.S. Pacific Fleet at its moorings in Pearl Harbor on the island of Oahu.

Fifty years have passed since the events I am about to relate took place. Despite the passage of time, it seems like yesterday. My mind sees clearly the shipmates I knew so well as they emerge, laughing and talking, from a hatch, port side, main deck, aft, of the *Oklahoma*. It is time for morning quarters for muster, and at the urging of their petty officers, the white-uniformed sailors good-naturedly form into double ranks. They stand at ease by the after gun turret, squaring round hats over suntanned faces, waiting for the arrival of their division officers.

I see and recognize each man, though the faces of some seem to be in shadow as if a cloud in the bright Hawaiian sky had sought them out by chance. As if aware of my presence, one of the sailors cast in shadow looks directly at me, smiling briefly in momentary recognition over the intervening years, then looks back at his companions. Their talk is animated and they turn in my direction. Then the cloud grows darker and I see those certain few less clearly.

The image fades as I look out over my native New England countryside, so far removed in geography and time. For me, those carefree American sailors standing there on the *Oklahoma*'s fantail are very real and will remain forever young, as I knew them in the peacetime days of 1940–41.

It is in memory of those brave and not so brave men who fought—and some who died—on that Sunday morning in Hawaii so far from home that I have written this account.

Acknowledgments

My thanks to the survivors of the *Oklahoma*'s turret no. 4 and some others, without whose recollections and contributions this account could not have been written. Former Chief Gunner's Mate Dick Whitman was kind enough to read the manuscript with a critical eye.

Particular thanks go to the late Gerald "Dutch" Foreman, a quartermaster in the *Oklahoma* and historian of the OKLAHOMA Association, for the use of material from his "Quartermaster's Notebook."

And to Paul Stillwell, formerly senior editor of the *U.S. Naval Institute Proceedings* and presently editor-in-chief of *Naval History*, for his encouragement and thorough reading of the first draft of the manuscript.

And also to a former sometime shipmate, the late Admiral Samuel Eliot Morison, distinguished naval historian and Harvard professor, for his help and understanding. We served together in the light cruiser *Honolulu* during several combat operations in the South Pacific, while he was researching and writing his history of the naval operations in World War II. I was a quartermaster petty officer, a member of ship's company. We formed a friendship that was renewed when we returned to Harvard after the war. Admiral Morison and Captain Herbert Rommel started me on the long process of writing this book, the latter by giving me the list of names of turret no. 4 personnel, the former by encouraging the Navy Department to supply the current addresses to match.

Trapped at Pearl Harbor

Prologue

The USS *Oklahoma* and most of the Pacific Fleet had been at sea on maneuvers and had only yesterday returned to port. It was the first time since the "Okie" had come out to Pearl Harbor earlier in the year that all the fleet battleships operating in the Hawaiian area had been ordered into port at the same time. On this first weekend in December there were eight in port, including Admiral Husband E. Kimmel's flagship *Pennsylvania*, currently in dry dock no. 1.

To many it didn't make much sense. As a precautionary measure it had been the practice to keep some of the heavy fleet units always at sea as tensions with Japan built up in the Far East.

Quartermaster Third Class John Gercevic had taken a peek at the officer of the deck's confidential file while standing a bridge watch at sea a few nights ago. He noticed an official message addressed to all ships and stations, "Be on the alert for Jap planes and subs."

Condition three antiaircraft gun watches—one watch in four—had been set for some weeks now while the ships were at sea. Live ammunition was kept in nearby ready boxes. Now, in port, all gun watches were secured except for a few machine gun security watches. Live ammunition was stored away under lock and key, in ready boxes and in the powder magazines below. The officer of the deck had custody of the keys; he was supposed to wear them around his neck where they would be readily available in any emergency.

Not only was the greater part of the fleet in port with guns secured, but a major fleet admiral's material inspection had been scheduled for this coming Monday, 8 December, the day after tomorrow. In the *Oklahoma*, this meant opening up all watertight compartments on the third deck and below—below the waterline—to the inspection teams. The usual practice—navy regs—on all ships whether at anchor or in port, was to set Condition Zed at the end of each working day. This meant that all watertight compartments were closed on the third deck and below. For the admiral's on the 8th, even the void spaces in the protective blisters that extended along the length of the ship at the waterline had been opened. The blisters were designed to absorb the explosions of torpedoes before they could penetrate the skin of the ship to do extensive damage. Some of the older hands commented that they could not remember such an inspection having been conducted before when ships were outside the continental limits of the United States. It was too dangerous, for ships were vulnerable to and could not contain any damage received from an enemy or by accidental internal explosion.

There was little, if any, watertight integrity in the *Oklahoma* this weekend. She was in a state of complete nonreadiness—despite the prospect of war with Japan in the near future.

Sailors also commented on the lack of early morning patrol plane activity. The huge, lumbering PBYs made an awful racket as they strained to rise off the waters near Ford Island to search the sea around Hawaii for any Japanese activity. But their search patterns for some reason did not cover the ocean northwest of Hawaii this weekend.

Whatever the reasoning behind these matters, or even who made the decisions, was not the sailors' concern; for we were not privy to information regarding reduced patrol plane activity, fleet operating schedules, admiral's inspections, and whether or not gun watches should be secured in port.

The usual watch and watch liberty port and starboard had been granted, allowing half of the crew to go ashore. Liberty expired on fleet landing at twelve midnight. The *Oklahoma*'s commanding officer, Captain Howard D. "King" Bode, U.S. Navy, late of the destroyer tender *Black Hawk* of the Asiatic Fleet, had already gone ashore.

The 4th division living space was located on the second deck below, port side, aft, just at the turn of the ship. It was home to sixty plus sailors and contained berthing, messing, and locker facilities. I slept in a top bunk in the middle of the compartment and my locker was just by the ladder that led topside to the main deck, aft. Showers and head were located just aft of the living compartment. A hatch up forward gave access to the Okie's ship's service compartment, which contained the ship's store and soda fountain, commonly called the "gedunk stand." Several twenty-four-inch portholes looked out over the water, open in port, dogged shut at sea.

General quarters is the navy's call for all hands to man their battle stations. Continuous drilling produced the quick and efficient manning of a ship about to go into battle. Each sailor had his battle station—on the bridge, in the engine rooms, on the guns, or standing by in damage control or sick bay. The highest degree of watertight integrity was set.

Of the more than sixty sailors in the 4th division, exactly fifty-six manned the 14-inch no. 4 gun turret at general quarters. There were also two turret officers.

The petty officers and seamen had battle stations down through the turret to the powder handling room four decks below. Mine was in the upper starboard powder hoist room. My companions there were fellow Seaman First Class Stanton Jones and Seaman Second Class Bill "Popeye" Schauf.

The inner workings of the turret were protected by a heavily armored barbette within which the turret revolved to train and fire its three guns. The face, sides, and top of the turret housing were shaped so that shot, shells, and bombs, would ricochet off the armored steel, whose thickness was designed to prevent the penetration of any known projectiles. The four gun turrets of the *Oklahoma*, because they contained the main battery, were the best protected areas in the ship during time of battle—from the upper turret down through the barbette to the powder magazines far below the waterline.*

An armored deck that constituted much of the second deck below gave the crew additional protection from projectiles and bombs. The next deck down, the third, was called the "splinter deck," designed to protect against any exploding metal fragments. The guns of turret no. 4 customarily faced aft and could be trained to port or starboard and elevated or lowered depending on range and bearing to the target.

The huge 1,400-pound armor-piercing or common projectiles were hoisted up into the gun chamber from the shell deck, where more than 150 of them, secured with light line, were standing upright around the bulkheads.† After being brought up to the gun chamber, the shells were lowered into projectile trays that were aligned with the open gun breeches. Rammermen then rammed the shells hydraulically into the breeches. Twelve 105-pound powder bags—four for each gun—were sent up the port and starboard powder hoists from the magazines and powder handling room four decks below. The powder bags were sent into the gun chamber from the hoist rooms after flameproof doors were opened to permit their passage. Four powder bags followed directly behind each projectile as it was rammed. The gun captains then closed the breeches and the guns were ready to fire.

During the recent short-range battle practice when the ship's four gun turrets had fired for record, the metal teeth of the hoist had bitten into one of the powder bags, spilling powder onto the powder tray and deck. Popeye Schauf had reacted quickly in the emergency, scooping up the loose powder pellets in his skivvy shirt and sending the lot along into the gun chamber to be fired off with the rest of the powder. Chief Turret Captain Maurice Brown had told Schauf he'd done a good job and that was enough for Popeye.

In general quarters the sailors could enter the turret from topside by ducking up into the control booth through a hatch underneath the turret

---

*Armor thickness of barbette—13 inches to second deck, 4¼ inches to third. Armor thickness, face of turret—18 inches; sides—9 inches; top—5 inches.

†The common shell is the same as the armor-piercing shell, except that it is not fitted with the soft steel cap and the metal of the shell is thinner, thus allowing a larger space and bursting charge. The armor-piercing shell can penetrate armor or concrete to a much greater degree.

overhang jutting back a few feet over the main deck and from there scramble into the gun chamber and down through the turret.

Or we could go below, down one ladder from the ship's service compartment through the shipfitter and carpenter shops on the third deck, around the outside of the barbette, then down another ladder to the first platform deck (one deck below the third deck) past the "Lucky Bag," and on through a heavy steel door into the powder handling room. Some stayed where they were; others climbed up through the turret to the shell deck, gun pits, gun chambers, and hoist rooms, stopping wherever they had battle stations.

The ship's Lucky Bag was the storage place for all clothing found adrift about the ship. The master-at-arms would periodically open it so sailors could claim their clothes. The Lucky Bag had also become the storage place for the crew's hammocks—mine was one—and in tropical waters, the sailors' peacoats, one of which belonged to me too. The Lucky Bag was one of the few places to be locked up tight despite Monday's scheduled material inspection.

PART 1

Turret No. 4

1

"*Oklahoma*, Last Call!" the coxswain yelled and the rest of the battle-ship *Oklahoma*'s Saturday night liberty party ran noisily down Pearl Harbor's fleet landing to pile into the fifty-foot motor launch that lay alongside, ready to take the late arrivals back to the ship. Liberty was up at midnight on the pier.

Other liberty boat coxswains from "Battleship Row" sounded off with their own ship calls: "*Arizona, West Virginia, California, Nevada, Tennessee, Maryland!*" they bellowed and the names of these powerfully gunned ships-of-the-line rolled and echoed along the smooth water of the harbor in the black night.

"OKLAHOMA, Last Call!" The coxswain shouted one last time.

"Sit down, damn it! Sit down in the boat!" he ordered the lurching, shoving sailors, many of whom were somewhat under the weather from a night in Honolulu. Others, like the beery trio of boatswain's mates second class Arthur Claudmantle and William "Shanghai" Walker and recently busted Seaman Ed Krames, had attended the "battle of the bands" at the new Bloch Recreational Center on the base. The battle-ship *Pennsylvania* had won the battle against stiff opposition from the other ships.

Finally, the two sailors who were the bow and stern hooks were told to cast off, and the launch headed out into the blackness of the harbor, its red and green running lights and white stern light showing its course and speed to other similarly lighted small craft as they made their own way home.

The night was warm and pleasant and the sleepy sailors looked around at the looming hulks of the great warships that lay at their anchorages or were moored to the concrete quays hard by Ford Island in the middle of the harbor. There was the *Oklahoma*, outboard of the *Maryland*.

The red aviation warning lights atop the masts probed the night sky above. The stars, brilliant in these tropical latitudes, shone down on the carefree, white-uniformed sailors to light their journey home. Occasionally a cloud drifted along the sky to come beween the sailors and the stars. And then it was gone.

The coxswain brought the launch alongside the *Oklahoma*'s after accommodation ladder, portside, and the liberty party began to go aboard.

"I saw those harbor lights; they only told me we were parting . . . ," a sailor sang mournfully.

"Shut up," advised the coxswain. "Take it easy, damn it." He worried

9

the last of the liberty party up the ladder to the quarterdeck. At last they were all on board and heading for their bunks.

"Shove off cox'n and secure for the night." The officer of the deck looked down at the tired petty officer at the launch's tiller.

"Aye, aye, Sir," the sailor saluted. "Cast off," he told the bow hook. The boat engineer put the engine slow ahead and the coxswain brought the launch around the stern of the ship where the crew secured it to the after boat boom. Then they too went aboard, swinging up the swaying Jacob's ladder and turned in to their bunks below.

Sailors who had not gone ashore that Saturday had already hit the sack. It would be an early reveille for those of us who were temporarily assigned as 4th division messcooks.

The 12 to 4, or midwatch as the navy called it—the first of the day— was already half-way gone. The ship was finally quiet, and except for the few on watch, or on overnight liberty, the rest of the 82 officers and 1,272 men of ship's company slept peacefully below.

It was Sunday, 7 December 1941.

2

J ohn Gercevic was tired when his midwatch drew to a close. As quartermaster of the watch, it seemed to him that he'd never had such a busy time of it, handling the noisy, beer-laden liberty parties returning to the ship. More problems than usual, he thought, even if it was just after payday.

As soon as he was relieved, Gercevic went below and turned in his bunk in the steering room, aft, for what remained of the night. He would sleep in late this morning.

At the same time Gercevic was being relieved, a sailor shook Seaman Second Class Bob Lewis awake back in the 4th division living compartment. It was 0330 and time to go on watch. All around him sailors were sleeping peacefully—more than sixty men. Each of the four deck divisions had a 14-inch gun turret manned by sixty sailors. Plus some other men were assigned to the 4th division—Cox'n Banks, some lookouts, a few others.

Lewis climbed out of his bunk reluctantly and dressed slowly in the blue glow of the night battle lights. He made a trip to the head, splashed water on his face in the washroom, and went topside to relieve the watch. Lewis would be standing a 0400–0600 security watch on a .30-caliber Lewis machine gun up on the boat deck this morning. It had no ammunition but was aptly named anyway, he thought.

Lewis relieved the sailor on watch. It was still dark but dawn was not that far off and at least there should be some early morning activity around the harbor to keep him awake, Lewis thought.

If the guns had no ready ammunition on hand, and that included everything on board from his .30-caliber Lewis to the antiaircraft, the broadside, and the main battery guns of the four turrets, then the ship was prepared for inspection, anyway, he said to himself. Everything on board had been scrubbed and shined, gallons of paint had been spread around, watertight compartments opened. All was shipshape and secure.

Ammunition for the guns was safely stored in the 14-inch, 5-inch, and 3-inch magazines. All firing locks had been removed from the antiaircraft and broadside batteries, taken apart, put in oily rags, and stored away awaiting admiral's inspection. Some antiaircraft ammunition was stored in nearby ready boxes under lock and key.

And now the first light of dawn came flooding over the Hawaiian Islands. Lewis could hear the navy PBY patrol planes warming up at the Naval Air Station on nearby Ford Island.

With sunrise approaching, the planes began to take off. Lewis watched them from his vantage point on the boat deck. These huge amphibians made a terrible noise as they taxied down the ramps into the water. Looking at the lumbering patrol craft making their take-off runs over the harbor, Lewis wondered how they'd ever get in the air. As a matter of fact, three of them had to taxi back and try again, he noted. That should wake everyone up on board the ships if they weren't awake already. Maybe the planes had too much fuel on board, he speculated.

Lewis had been surprised to see so little patrol plane activity this morning—fewer planes in the air than had been the case since the Okie had returned to Pearl from San Francisco a couple of months ago. Why? Probably because it was Sunday, he figured.

Now the sun was up. The early morning running boats from the ships began to crisscross the harbor. Lewis looked over toward Pearl City and watched the color come over the land beyond as the day was born. Below him a sleepy boat crew made its way slowly across the main deck, aft. The sailors climbed out along the boat boom to drop into the motor launch beneath them.

Lewis was getting hungry. He stretched slowly. What was for chow this morning? Hot cakes and bacon, he thought.

Down in the living compartment, the five of us who were messcooking were already up, a half-hour before reveille went at 0600. The others were Mike Savarese, "Shadow" Bergstrom, Clarence Mullaley, and Dan Weissman.

I looked out a porthole across the harbor. It would be a great day to go to the beach. We kidded around some, then went up the ladder topside on our way to the galley, amidship, to get hot coffee for the division sailors who would be up and about this Sunday morning. We stopped on the main deck, aft, for a few minutes and gazed around the harbor.

I looked down the line of Battleship Row and over at the *Maryland,* waving at a couple of sailors standing on the fantail. Some life was beginning to stir about the decks of those huge warships of the Pacific Fleet. Glancing up, I saw the rising sun touch the peaks of the Waianae Mountains behind the harbor to the north. All seemed peaceful and secure in our sailors' world.

It was quiet now that the PBYs had flown off to patrol their assigned sectors to the south and southwest. None would patrol the seas to the north or northwest this morning though we had no way of knowing this. There were rumors—"scuttlebutt" to the sailors—about the ship that Japanese aircraft and submarines were operating in the Hawaiian Islands area.

We weren't worried. It was going to be warm and sunny, one of those perfect days for which the islands were famous. A few early morning fair-weather clouds moved slowly across a bright blue sky. A light trade wind barely rippled the placid waters of the harbor as it moved gently across its surface.

Lewis passed us as he went below. He said he was hungry. We went up the ladder to the galley, got pots of steaming coffee from the cooks, and went back below to the 4th division living compartment.

3

Cox'n Al Sandall was in charge of the 4th division topside crew this morning. The wooden deck would receive a "clamp-down" only with wet swabs. Bob Lewis, who had just gone below, was sent back up again to help out. Breakfast would be piped down at 0700.

Sandall had a tough time getting the sleepy sailors going. Some had had a rousing time of it in town last night. Before heading back to the ship, more than a few had stopped for one last one at the Black Cat Café on King Street, across from the more sedate Army and Navy YMCA. A pair of boxing gloves painted on the door of this frolicking, rollicking watering spot fascinated Shadow Bergstrom. The navy's shore patrol stopped by frequently.

The boatswain's mate of the watch shrilled his bos'n's pipe and passed the word over the ship's announcing system (except in officers' country): "Now hear this. Clean sweep-down, fore and aft; empty all trash cans and spit kits." ("Spit kits" were round, shallow receptacles, relics of a bygone era, attached to stanchions throughout the ship. Designed for tobacco chewers like "Popeye" Schauf.) Even though the crew was permitted to sleep in an hour late because it was Sunday, the routine work of the ship must be done.

Russ Davenport, nicknamed "Pinky" for reasons best forgotten, and Jack Miller, another irrepressible type, were members of the duty boat crew. Once, while on a rousing liberty in Bremerton, Miller had found it necessary to appropriate an Indian blanket to replace his missing uniform. The reason is also best forgotten. They went topside, crossed the fantail, walked out along the boat boom, then swung down the Jacob's ladder to drop easily into the fifty-foot motor launch.

The boat had already made an early run into fleet landing for odds and ends, some fresh milk and vegetables, the Sunday papers. The two sailors puttered around in the boat, waiting to be called away for another run, probably with a church party this time.

Seaman Second Class Harold Johnson was standing by his bunk in his skivvies, giving his shoes a last-minute shine. He was getting ready to go on liberty and had his shore-going whites laid out neatly on his bunk.

A friend from back home in the state of Washington had been standing a watch with him last week in the enclosed lookout station atop the mainmast. The sailor asked Johnson if he'd seen the article in *Life* magazine about the Japanese Navy. His friend was of the opinion that the U.S. Navy could take the Japs in nothing flat. Johnson said no, he figured it would take a couple of years. It was idle chit-chat to pass the time away on watch.

The war in Europe, North Africa, and the Far East seemed so far away, and indeed it was—for the time being. Most of us spent little time thinking about these things, for we were young, fully taken up in life at the moment and the pursuit of happiness. We were reminded of world affairs only occasionally when, for example, we might walk by a Japanese merchant ship docked in Honolulu and catch the eyes of the Japanese sailors looking impassively down at us. Neither group would acknowledge the other. But I think we all somehow guessed what lay ahead of us.

A few months ago, the Royal Navy's HMS *Warspite*, severely damaged by Nazi dive-bombers in the battle for Crete had limped into Pearl on the way to the States for repairs. There had been many casualties among her crew. The year before this proud battleship had fought the Germans off Norway's northern capes.

It was the first time for most of us that the war had been brought home to our sailor's world. Some of us visited our counterparts in the *Warspite,* where the British sailors showed us the damaged casemates and took us down through the turrets. They were young like us, but no longer innocent.

And now, when drilling at night battle stations in turret no. 4, I wondered what it would be like to go into action against Nazi dive-bombers or the Imperial Japanese Fleet. Would the ship survive? Would there be dead and wounded sailors?

Cox'n Bob Roberts was sitting on his bunk reading the comics in the *Honolulu Advertiser.* The bronzed boat coxswain yawned—at peace with the world this Sunday morning.

A sailor named Francis Skifnes came down the ladder and called for Frank Scott. He was from the *Maryland,* which was tied up inboard and he had come over to visit his friend Scott.

Scott said, "Francis, I've got duty in the boat in a few minutes; I've got to get out there and start getting ready for the morning liberty runs."

"We've got time for some acey-deucey, a game anyway," Skifnes insisted.

They went back to Scott's bunk, broke out the acey-deucey board, sat down on the bunk, and rolled the dice.

The boat coxswain came along and told Scott to come on, let's get out in the boat and clean it up.

Scott said, "Just a minute. Let's finish the game, and I'll get out there."

He looked out the porthole next to his bunk. "It's going to be a nice day, Francis."

Scott had told me how he'd come to be assigned to the Okie. He had gone through the Great Lakes boot camp with a friend from home, Harry Nichols. Nichols was also on board the ship, a storekeeper third class.

"Nichols and I were wondering what we would put in for, what kind of ship. The training station had this large-size model of a battleship for us boots to look at, and it happened to be the *Oklahoma.*

"I said to Harry, 'Look at the stern of that ship. See those big portholes? If the ship ever sinks and we have to get out, then we go out through them. They look big enough to squeeze through.' "

The two boots had put in for the Okie and got their wish. And, in Scott's case, by coincidence, he was given a bunk near one of the ports in the stern of the ship that had attracted his attention back at Great Lakes.

Following breakfast, Norman Wiley, a gunner's mate striker in the turret, went up the ladder topside and stood by the 4th division hatch. He would get some fresh air for a few minutes before going back to work in the turret in preparation for tomorrow's inspection. He looked around the harbor. The massive bulk of the turret loomed behind him.

Rufus Nance, boatswain's mate second class, stood in front of his locker down in the living compartment. He had recently broken his finger. It was in a splint and it hurt. There was some work to do but he could order the seamen around and therefore the finger shouldn't bother him. He might even go ashore.

Nance was not the only walking casualty in the division this morning. Big Chuck Holzhauer, sometimes called "Happy," was limping around, the victim of one of Stanton Jones's practical jokes.

Jones had seen Holzhauer sleeping soundly in his top bunk one morning just before reveille. Holzhauer was lying on his back, blissfully snoring, with one of his legs hanging over the edge of the bunk. Jones got some light line, tiptoed over to the sleeping sailor, made a loop around Holzhauer's big toe, then tied the line to the bunk chain. He stood back to see what would happen when the bugler sounded reveille and Holzhauer got out of his bunk. The rest of us were now watching this bit of horseplay. The bugle blared forth. The word was passed, "Reveille, reveille; all hands heave out and lash up!"

Holzhauer was already lashed up. He woke up and swung over the edge of his bunk to drop to the deck. He got himself hung up by his big toe. Everybody roared. Except Happy Holzhauer, who for some reason didn't appreciate the humor of hanging from his bunk, head down, grabbing frantically for support, toe tied to bunk chain. Sympathetic hands helped extricate him from his predicament. That morning he was anything but happy. He could really have hurt himself.

Holzhauer asked Jones if he knew anything about it and Jones said no. Holzhauer had been hopping around the compartment lately, babying his toe. He supposed he was still lucky to have it, sprained or otherwise. But he never did find out who liked him well enough to hang him up by his big toe like that.

Then there was Leon "Snuffy" Arickx. He had this messy habit of sticking pinches of snuff under his lower lip and sort of leering out at you. We all told him it was disgusting and of course he paid no attention to us. We wondered how his assorted girl friends dealt with it.

Snuffy had just been "double" tattooed, the first time one night in Honolulu after putting away several zombies, a most lethal drink. (They cost an expensive full dollar when seamen earned only thirty-six or fifty-four dollars per month.) The tattoo was of a naked girl—in detail. Snuffy was proud of this masterpiece.

The fatherly Captain Edward J. Foy, a favorite of the crew, had spotted Snuffy's new tattoo at the next Saturday's personnel inspection. He gave Snuffy a "dressing down" for his bad taste and ordered him to dress up the lady. Snuffy went ashore and got a dress tattooed over the naked girl to suit the skipper's desire for modesty. It was still healing.

Now the *Oklahoma* had a new commanding officer, Captain Howard D. "King" Bode, late of the Asiatic Fleet. He was already earning a reputation—one that prompted the junior officers to hang irreverent names on him like "Flower Pot" or "Captain Bligh."

He's "Asiatic" as hell, said the enlisted men, meaning not quite up to specifications. It covered a bit of ground. And water. But whatever the crew thought of him, he was the captain. He had not returned aboard as yet this Sunday morning.

The last of the ambulatories was John "Hutch" Wortham. He was traveling barefoot as much as he could these days. He had a pig tattoo on one instep and a rooster on the other. They were still brightly colored new and Wortham was staying away from socks and shoes as much as he could.

Wortham acknowledged our greetings by sticking the knuckle joint of a missing finger against one nostril of his nose. It looked terrible; as if he had the whole finger up his nose. He looked so idiotic, we had to laugh.

This gunner's mate second class had accidentally had his finger chopped off in the turret powder hoist awhile back. Clayton McQuay was running the hoist and thought "all hands" were clear when he started it up. Wortham, cleaning rag in hand, had reached into the hoist with a glob of grease just at that moment. "Hold it!" someone yelled, but it was too late. The hoist went down instead of up. And Wortham was missing two joints on the middle finger of his right hand. He swore feelingly and was sent off to sickbay for repairs. Mike Saverese, who was striking for gunner's mate, got the job of fishing the missing digit out of the hoist. Over the side.

Wortham didn't tell his wife back in L.A. He said when he got home he'd stick the stub of his finger in his ear to see what she'd say. He was married to an Italian girl named Mary and they had a baby son.

Wortham couldn't swim and had been worrying about it lately. So he decided to do something about it and had gone ashore in Honolulu one night and gotten a rooster tattooed on the upper instep of one foot and a pig on the other.

There was an old navy superstition that these two tattoos, one on each foot, would prevent a man from drowning. This done, although a painful project, made Wortham feel better. His wife and son would be protected if something should happen. He listened to some good-natured kidding—"Cock-a-doodle do" and "oink-oink." He laughed and disappeared up the ladder.

"So long, Hutch," we said. "Stay away from the water."

4
~~

Arthur Claudmantle had a headache. It was not surprising considering last night's beer-drinking shore excursion with Shanghai Walker and Ed Krames. Krames and Walker were down below sleeping it off in an out-of-the-way blower space. Claudmantle took a shower, drank some coffee, and felt better. As a matter of fact, he felt like going ashore again and, deciding his erstwhile shore-going companions had slept long enough, he went below to get them up. He couldn't rouse them so he too stretched out for a rest. There was no hurry.

Seaman Second Class Everett Gunning was dressed for liberty. He was on his way to the print shop to borrow some paper clips so that he could pin back his bell bottoms. It was against regulations to wear anything but the straight up and down issue trousers to go ashore, but many of the sailors managed the bell bottoms, which had a bit more flair. He was going swimming today with a nice Hawaiian girl named Eleanor who happened to have seven names in all. He knew the first and last but had trouble with the other five. It didn't matter.

Edward "Curly" Slapikas, seaman first, was also going ashore. We had gone through boot camp together. As befitting his "advanced age," he avoided dashing about the living space in any great state of excitement. He had learned that if one moved around in a leisurely, organized manner, one was as likely to catch the same early liberty boat as the others. He stepped carefully into his whites and his newly shined shoes, knotted his neckerchief and turned to speak to William P. "Popeye" Schauf, who was standing near the 4th division ladder, contentedly puffing on a cigar. He told his friend he was glad to see him going to church.

Popeye looked suspiciously at the balding Slapikas. Was Slapikas being sarcastic? Slapikas had gotten him in trouble a few months ago when Popeye had asked him to write a letter of introduction to a girl he'd never met. Slapikas reluctantly did him the favor and had used a lot of fancy words. When Popeye met the girl in a Honolulu bar, she knew he wasn't the same person by the way he talked and she decided to leave. She became upset when Popeye tried to kiss her goodnight. The evening was a bit of a disaster.

When Popeye reported in, he accused Slapikas of betraying him with all those big words. Slapikas just groaned and rolled his eyes at the overhead. It was his nature to extend a helping hand to the younger sailors and we appreciated his friendly interest. Popeye Schauf frustrated him.

Popeye said that he always went to church on Sundays. Although the Catholic chaplain, Lieutenant Junior Grade Aloysius H. Schmitt, regularly held church services on board, Popeye had decided to go to Mass ashore today.

"We hope you go to confession, too, Popeye," yelled Mike Saverese.

"I don't have nothin' to confess, Saverese, except I'd like to pop you one."

"Oh ho, Popeye the sailor is feeling tough this morning!" The happy-go-lucky Mike would torment Popeye from time to time by sneaking up behind him and patting his cheeks together when Popeye had worked up a good chew, then dance away. Popeye would choke and cough, trying not to swallow the tobacco juice, and his eyes would bulge. He'd threaten to spit all over the grinning Saverese the next time he did that. But of course he didn't. They liked each other.

Popeye grinned. Let them kid him all they wanted to. He'd just bought a box of cigars at the ship's store yesterday and he had plenty of chewing tobacco on hand. And after church, he might just go on into town for a few beers.

So what's wrong with that, he thought. Popeye didn't plan on getting rid of his cigar when he saluted the officer of the deck and went over the side into the motor launch. He would palm it in his left hand, then light it up again when they hit fleet landing.

Wilbur T. "Wimpy" Hinsperger sat at one of the mess tables drinking coffee. We told him he was drinking too much beer. "You look like a bowling ball," we teased.

"Doc" Savage joined the group. "You're getting pudgy too," we told him. "You're eating too many veal chops." Savage smiled. We went back to boot camp, too. I liked him.

The barefoot Bruce Spaulding, long a seaman and now a coxswain, was padding around the compartment trying to make up his mind what time he'd hit the beach. Full of the joy of living, the only thing that seemed to bother Spaulding was that the navy made him wear shoes from time to time. He was more comfortable without them.

Seaman Marion Athas made his way topside to stand on the main deck, aft, near the plane catapult. He too was dressed to go ashore and was waiting for "liberty call." He looked up at the observation seaplane, an OS2U, snugly secured on the catapult and idly wondered what it would be like to fly one.

Down below on the third deck, where Claudmantle and his friends were "flaked out," a game of dominoes was taking place in the master-at-arms shack, as was the custom on a Sunday morning.

Stanton Jones was an observer. He was walking around the game, breaking in a pair of shoes he'd just bought. They were to be used for liberties and personnel inspections.

The players, who were trying to concentrate, complained to Jones that his shoes were squeaking, distracting their thought processes. Jones grinned and continued his squeaking promenade.

Back in the living compartment, Bob Lewis finished breakfast, got up from the mess table, and lay down on his bunk with the comic section of the Sunday paper. Eating across from him at the table this morning was another seaman, named Alvin Brown. The two hadn't talked much. Lewis didn't like Brown, and Brown apparently felt the same about Lewis.

Al Sandall, done with his topside duties and up from the breakfast table, tried to wake his friend Coxswain Layton Banks. Banks was a favorite of the division officer, Ensign Rommel. We teased him by calling him "teacher's pet." He retaliated by telling us he was going to drive us all "over the hill" when he made cox'n.

Banks was in charge of the ship's lamp locker, on the second deck just aft of the 4th division head. It was the storage place for the portable running lights for the ship's small boats. When Banks got married two months ago outside Reno during the Okie's stay in San Francisco, he had asked Sandall to stand up for him and Sandall had. Banks was a sound sleeper and when Sandall tried to shake him awake, he just groaned. "Reveille! C'mon, Banks, get up. Rise and shine!"

Sandall finally grabbed Banks by the legs and pulled him out of the bunk. Banks got up.

"C'mon, let's go ashore," Sandall said. Banks gave him some guff for roughhousing him awake.

"Lay off, Al; I'm not going anywhere yet. I'm going back to the lamp locker to sleep some more," he said.

Sandall gave up, and Banks got dressed and headed aft through the living compartment and out of sight.

Others were busy going and coming to the head, showers, topside, and on neighborly visits to shipmates in the area.

The newly promoted Westley Potts, now a boatswain's mate second class, was moving around the compartment. He was a member of the ship's pistol team and sometimes drew the ammunition when he and Ensign Rommel, also a member, went ashore to shoot. Also on the Okie's boxing squad, Cox'n Potts had been petty officer in charge of the 4th division living space and the powder handling room when I reported on board over a year ago.

Also recently promoted—to gunner's mate second class—was the likeable Dick Whitman, sometimes called "Gopher-puss" by Chief Turret Captain Maurice M. "Molly" Brown. Brown was the senior enlisted man in turret no. 4. Whitman had been a rammerman in the turret during general quarters. Now he was the turret trainer; it was worth another three dollars a month to him.

Seaman First Dan Weissman, fellow messcook, was anxious to hit the beach. In fact, it was becoming an obsession—this fascination for going on liberty. Dan had recently discovered that there was more to life than staying on board ship and going to the movies. Now you couldn't keep him away from the various temptations ashore. Even when he didn't rate liberty, he was after someone to stand by for him. This rapidly developing social life had improved Weissman's disposition and performance of duty we told him. And it had. Dan smiled nowadays; he was a pretty good guy. He was another sailor in the 4th division who couldn't swim.

"Hey, Curly, how long do you figure we'll be out here in Pearl?" we asked.

"Forever," Slapikas replied.

5

One of the division's favorite petty officers was blond and balding "Oley" Oleson. He related to everyone, chiefs and seamen. Oley had replaced another favorite turret captain, Roy Stewart, who had gone up to turret no. 2.

The popular Oleson was a small man physically—five feet tall. He told us he had to stretch to get into the navy and we believed him—sort of. He was a big man in most everything else. He had never learned to swim and was teased about this shortcoming from time to time.

Mike Saverese asked him why he wore his uniforms so big. Oleson replied that the brass liked to see you in baggy clothes—just so long as they're clean.

"Why do you put pepper all over you food like that?" Oleson would ask and Mike would say it's because he was brought up that way. "You have a strange accent, Savarese," Oleson would inform the grinning sailor from Brooklyn.

Oleson kept his inspection shoes in a pair of socks to protect them from the elements. At Saturday morning personnel inspection, Oley would fish the shoes out of his locker and carry them topside. Proceeding in his stocking feet to his assigned station, he'd carefully set the gleaming black shoes down on the wooden deck, heels together, toes 45 degrees apart, in the position of attention. Then he'd step slowly and easily into them. Of course, the whole division would be watching him by this time, eyes drawn to those shining shoes, which sparkled brightly in the morning sun. They must be two sizes too big, we thought. Oleson completely ignored us.

When the captain passed down the ranks, he would always compliment Oleson on his shoes and ignore his baggy dress uniform. Oleson would smile and thank the captain. When the inspection was over and we secured from quarters, Oley reversed the procedure and the shoes went back in his locker to await next week's inspection. We thought this was a pretty nifty trick. There was nothing like a pair of well-shined shoes to distract a critical inspection party.

Louis C. "Red" Templeton, the division bos'n's mate, was another kind. He thought he was a tough guy. You had to watch him. Various of his shipmates, past and present, had run afoul of this belligerent first class petty officer.

Clarence Mullaley remembered in his Texas drawl, "Old Red gettin' a good lick or two" coming back to the ship in the liberty boat one night.

"He'd been drinkin' and when the bow hook told him, 'Let's go, Red, get in the boat so we can cast off,' Old Red tried to land one on him. The bow hook knocked him 'ass over teakettle.' When the boat came alongside the gangway, Red tried to 'sucker punch' the bow hook. The guy knocked Old Red on his ass for good this time."

"I remember how Red wouldn't get out of his sack the next morning and Claudmantle was the only one that dared go near him and tell him it was time to get up. You should have seen the black eye he had."

"The bow hook was a quiet, good-looking guy named Dubois," Dick Whitman said. "Both of them got put on report and Red went up to Captain's Mast. The skipper said to Red to go ashore and drink some more so he could learn how to handle it."

"What's with that guy, anyway? I heard Roy Stewart, the turret captain, tell Red he was going to deck him if he didn't shut up. I don't know what it was all about. Red didn't want to tangle with Roy and he backed off," Whitman said.

"He's like a lot of small guys," said a sailor. "Wants to prove how tough he is all the time. Always got a chip on his shoulder. Plus he's a red head and they got mean tempers." The stereotypes were offered as explanation.

"Oley Oleson's short too," someone reminded us. "And Stewart."

We agreed they were a lot different than Templeton and we tried to steer clear of the 4th division's bandy-legged boatswain's mate. It wasn't easy.

Pinky Davenport had his own story. "I was sitting in this bar in town minding my own business and drinking a zombie. I look around and just then in comes Red and heads straight for me. "Well, those big red freckles are just jumpin' out all over his face and he's got his hat jammed down over his eyes—like this—and I figure he looks kind of wild and he's lookin' at me.

"All of a sudden he starts cussin' away at me for no reason that I know of. Everyone's looking our way and I can hear all that Hawaiian music in the background and I say, 'Knock it off, Red; you're not on the ship now. My money is as good as yours.' "

Davenport went on. "Red grabbed at me so I let him have it—punched him in the kisser as hard as I could. Decked his ass out cold." Russ had big hands; when doubled up, they produced huge fists. "So the bouncer comes over and throws me out of the place; Red was still out of it, there on the deck . . . and he don't look so full of piss and vinegar anymore."

"What did you do then?"

"Nothin'. I made a couple more bars and ran into my good buddy Frank Scott and told him about it. Frank told me I was in for it now and he was right. Templeton put me on every working party he could think of. But Mr. Rommel finally stepped in when I squawked that this bullshit had gone on long enough and he gave me my own cleaning station to take care of. I guess it's okay now 'cause Rommel complimented me a couple times and now I'm in the boat. I still don't know what got into Red that night and you can bet your ass I don't trust him now," the young seaman finished.

Most of the division sailors did not trust Templeton or like him very much. His fellow petty officers shunned him for the most part.

"You know Red sometimes carries a dog pin in his hand; it's like carrying a roll of nickels and if he pops you, you've had it—a broken jaw, maybe," one of the petty officers said.

The prim and proper Ensign Rommel and the cocky, foul-mouthed Templeton were close. Rommel depended on Templeton to run the deck end of the division however he chose, not wanting to hear of problems unless forced upon him. It was an odd relationship; the two were such different personalities. One, the reserved and rather prissy young reserve officer—tall and handsome in his dress uniform; the other, a scrappy little red-headed petty officer of the "old navy" who by his nature trusted no officer, least of all a "thirty-day wonder."

Ensign Rommel did make an effort towards the men, though sometimes his somewhat awkward attempts at friendship seemed a bit stuffy to us. Sincere or not, he did display an interest in the welfare of the division sailors. He liked to sail and occasionally invited one or the other of us to go along. He was finding his way. The navy was not exactly a democratic society; there was a great gap between the officers and enlisted men. Neither group quite trusted the other. Some progress was being made as college-trained reserve officers came into the fleet and better trained and educated young sailors filled out the enlisted ranks. In his own way, Rommel was trying to bridge the gap.

In Bremerton, the conscientious Rommel, then the assistant 4th division officer, had been standing an in-port OOD watch. Only recently reported on board for duty, he had checked out a civilian vendor coming on board with supplies—cans of this, jars of that—for the wardroom mess, as the officer of the deck is supposed to do. He had found the vendor to be short on one of his invoices and seemed quite proud to have spotted the discrepancy. The vendor was called to account and the matter straightened out. Fussy or not, Mr. Rommel had done what he was supposed to do.

Things did not always run smoothly, or happily, on the quarterdeck. Seaman A. L. Ellis, quartermaster striker, hated to stand watches with Ensign Rommel. "Thinks he's God on the quarterdeck," Al complained. "Always testing us on navy regs, tries to trip us up. Picky."

Al was a good, level-headed sailor. He was expressing his opinion. "Rommel's always bragging, saying his father was a captain or admiral or something. Has his nose up in the air all the time."

"He's okay, seems to be anyway, with the 4th division sailors," I said.

Now Ensign Rommel was preparing to go ashore to shoot in a police pistol match scheduled for today. He had already drawn his .45-caliber pistol and had put it in the safe in his stateroom. He dressed in his spotless, high-collared dress whites, the uniform of the day, with white shoes. He would have breakfast in the wardroom before leaving the ship. Looking at the .45 he'd just removed from the safe, Rommel wondered how he'd do in today's competition. He would be firing for the record. He worried about it some.

The blue and white PREP flag, indicating colors in five minutes, was being readied to be run up the yardarm hoist at 0755. When PREP was hauled down at 0800, the bugler would sound attention, the colors would be hoisted at the flagstaff on the fantail, and the Union Jack to the jack staff on the bow.

At the same time, the Okie's band, which was even now assembling on the main deck, aft, would sound off with the national anthem. All ships present in the harbor would perform this daily evolution simultaneously, guided by the PREP flag of the SOPA (senior officer present afloat) in the minesweeper *Oglala,* outboard of the light cruiser *Helena* at 1010 dock in the navy yard. All hands on deck would turn to the colors, aft, and salute in this time-honored navy tradition. The band performed this function daily in port. The musicians were enthusiastic and some were talented. The band gave frequent concerts for the crew on the main deck, aft, and played at officers' dances. Some band members had battle stations in the turret powder magazines.

Flying over the colors today, Sunday, and the only flag or pennant permitted to do so per navy regulations, would be the church pennant when church call sounded in a few minutes. It contained a blue cross— horizontal on a white field—and would be lowered when church services were over.

Chaplain Schmitt prepared for Mass. His battle station was in the *Oklahoma*'s sickbay, where he could comfort any wounded brought there in time of battle. He hoped the day would never come.

Cox'n Al Sandall said, "I think I'll go listen to some records," and he went up to the forward end of the compartment to listen to the new record player we had all chipped in to buy. Someone put on one of the current hits, "Let Me Off Uptown."

Down in the 4th division living compartment, Dick Whitman had finished breakfast. Most of the turret was ready for tomorrow's inspection, but there was still some work to do in the gun pits and Whitman was in charge. "I'm going up to the turret and get things started," Whitman told the other gunner's mates and strikers. "Then you come up." And he left. It was 0750.

PART 2

Air Raid,
Pearl Harbor!
This Is No Drill!

6

"**M**an the antiaircraft batteries! Man the antiaircraft batteries!"
The voice coming over the ship's general announcing system—impersonal but urgent—demanded immediate attention. And obedience.

Stunned by this unexpected call to antiaircraft battle stations, sailors on deck and in the living and working spaces throughout the ship stopped short in whatever they were doing—walking, talking, shaving, showering. We were mentally unprepared for this call to battle stations; we had been expecting more peaceful calls this morning. We looked at each other, momentarily frozen in place, trying to digest the meaning behind the words we heard.

What is this? Drills on Sunday? In port? asked a thousand incredulous voices and pairs of eyes.

What the hell is going on? The unanswered questions echoed through the length and breadth of the great battleship—from bridge to engine room, from wardroom to the 4th division living compartment on the second deck below.

Almost at once, the sailors who manned the antiaircraft batteries—the 5-inch, 3-inch, and machine guns—and the supporting stations—magazines, powder hoists, and fire control—were on the way, galvanized into action by the words coming over the announcing system.

Others who had battle stations on the bridge, in sick bay, and damage control, were also moving. Dressed in the uniform of the day of skivvy shirts and shorts, clean, white liberty uniforms—and a few in dungarees—they scrambled for ladders leading upward to their guns, or below to the powder magazines.

One of the few on board who saw what was happening just before the word was passed was Pinky Davenport, who was out in the motor launch secured to the after boat boom.

Planes were dropping bombs on Ford Island! Our planes? They had to be? How else could you account for it? What the hell were they doing? There were explosions! Smoke puffed up in the air.

Inside Turret 4, Dick Whitman heard nothing. He sat in the pointer's seat in order to elevate the guns so he could wipe and polish the recoil cylinders.

None of us in the 4th division living compartment were directly affected by this call to man the antiaircraft batteries. Our battle stations were in the turret, whose 14-inch guns by no stretch of the imagination could be used as antiaircraft weapons. Nevertheless, because anything that affected the ship in some way affected us, we stood rooted to the deck for the moment, startled by what we had just heard.

I was standing by my mess table, others by their lockers. Sailors sat up straight where they were relaxing in their bunks or on the shiny black seats of the 4th division head.

What was happening? Is it just a drill? Yes, but wait! The voice that had passed the word had sounded tense, excited; it was warning us of something else—but what?

Popeye Schauf took the cigar out of his mouth; the smoke of his last puff drifted though the living compartment. He couldn't think what all this meant. He'd be late for Mass if they fooled around this way.

A few of the sailors, the initial shock having passed, lay back in their bunks with the newspaper or to read a letter from home. Others continued their preparations to go on liberty. A sailor sitting in the head returned to his comic book; another turned his shower on, reaching for the soap.

Marion Athas, standing by the plane secured atop the catapult, looked out over the harbor and saw some low-flying planes heading towards Battleship Row from the direction of Merry Point. A mock attack by our own planes . . . the thought passed quickly through his mind.

Fascinated, he watched the planes grow larger as they headed straight in, skimming the placid water of the harbor.

The musicians in the bank broke ranks and took off in all directions, all thoughts of a musical performance gone from their minds.

Standing near the 3-inch/50-caliber antiaircraft gun just forward of the quarterdeck was Norman Wiley. Near him stood a ship's cook named Acker catching a breath of fresh air now that breakfast was over.

Jack Miller was just hoisting a leg over the lifeline on the fantail, coming up on deck from the motor launch tied up astern, when he heard the alarm. He looked to port, towards fleet landing, and saw the planes. Were his eyes playing tricks on him? It was pretty realistic.

Rufus Nance, standing by his locker down below, heard someone say, "A carrier must be coming in; the planes are simulating an air attack."

Up forward, in officers' country, Ensign Herb Rommel, the 4th division officer, heard the explosions and the alarm calling away the men to man the AA batteries. He ran out on deck. Somehow he knew what was happening. An old navy chief had warned him about the danger of having ships lined up like targets in the harbor. He saw a torpedo plane heading right for the ship.

"General Quarters! General Quarters!"

"All hands, man your battle stations! All hands, man your battle stations!" The words, jumping with danger and excitement, rang out loud and clear into every nook and cranny of the ship, searching out each sailor. *Bong-Bong, Bong-Bong,* went the general alarm. The ringing notes bounced along the passageways and up and down the ladders.

The call to general quarters was what it was all about—the one real reason for the navy's being. A chill ran along my spine. I could feel the blood rush fast through my veins. The bugle call sending a ship's crew to general quarters to man battle stations was the most urgent, demanding call in the navy. Once heard, it was never forgotten. Like Taps.

Following so fast on the first call to action, it came as a double shock. I couldn't believe, couldn't accept what I was hearing. My mind tried to understand the meaning. For a moment, the ship seemed deathly quiet . . . only the record player spun on and on.

I couldn't move. The other sailors couldn't either. Our bodies, trained for so long to react quickly in emergencies, refused to budge for those first few seconds, in shock from what we had heard. We tensed with the strain of listening. What next?

Running aft along the deck, Ensign Rommel heard the call to general quarters as he passed the quarterdeck. He saw a torpedo from one of the attacking planes slam into a cruiser at 1010 dock.*

With considerable presence of mind, Rommel jumped over to the general announcing system. He would try to get things moving. This was no drill! It was the real thing! He had to convince the ship it was under attack.

"This is no shit, God damn it! They're real bombs! A cruiser has just been sunk! Now get going!" Rommel's voice sounded over every speaker in the ship. I recognized his voice; some others did. I was shocked to hear such nonregulation expressions used over the ship's 1MC, and from Rommel of all people. But it got us moving. Now we had some idea of what was happening although we didn't have time to think about it.

The quarterdeck watch was stunned. The OOD, Lieutenant Sid Sherwin, fumbled around trying to come up with the keys to the ammunition ready boxes and magazines.

Air raid, Pearl Harbor! This was no drill!

*The cruiser *Helena* was damaged, not sunk.

7

E nsign Rommel, who only a few minutes before had been ready to leave the ship in his dress whites with his .45 to shoot in the pistol match ashore, ran along the deck to man his battle station in the control booth of turret no. 4. Ensign Joe Spitler from Texas, the assistant turret officer, should be right along.

Westley Potts was halfway up the division ladder when he heard Rommel pass the word. He scrambled out of the hatch and ran across the deck, moving as fast as he could . . . he thought. A bomb exploded in the water about two hundred yards from the ship, port side. Out of the corner of his eye, he could see torpedo planes swooping in across the harbor toward Battleship Row. He could see them releasing torpedos.

His speed across the deck increased and he ducked under the overhang and up the ladder into the booth in record time. Potts thought to himself that he didn't even bump his shins this time, he'd gotten up inside so fast. In the comparative safety of the turret, Potts manned his station on no. 3 gun and awaited developments.

Popeye Schauf heard the call to general quarters; he'd have to move. He took another puff on his cigar, then ran up the ladder, across the deck, and over to the turret. He couldn't take the lighted cigar inside, he knew, so he carefully laid it on an angle iron running around the outside of the barbette. He'd relight it when he came back outside, after all this was over, he thought. And he sure didn't want to go in the turret with his clean whites on and crawl around in that upper powder hoist room. But it looked like he had to. "The hell with it," Popeye said.

Just at that moment, Rommel came pounding up. "Get inside the turret," he shouted. "Get below decks; we can't fire the 14-inch guns anyway. You'll be safe from the bombs down there."

Marion Athas was already inside, crawling to his battle station in the upper left powder hoist room, where he was shortly joined by another sailor.

Even then, before the crew arrived at battle stations and watertight doors could be closed, the first torpedo plane was dropping its "fish" into the water. The torpedo was set to run shallow but to explode beneath the *Oklahoma's* armored belt, where it would do maximum damage. The U.S. Navy had no idea the Japanese had anything like it.

Now, at Rommel's urging, Popeye ducked under the overhang of the turret and climbed inside. Rommel came in right after him. Their dress whites would have to get dirty.

Wes Potts looked at Rommel, who was wearing his .45 pistol and gun belt. Regulations prohibited .45's hanging around inside the turret, so Potts figured Rommel must be the officer of the deck—the only officer in the ship who would be authorized to wear belt and pistol. And he'd heard Rommel pass the word. Rommel wasn't the OOD, of course; it was Lieutenant Sid Sherwin.

Rommel asked the men inside the turret, "Did you hear the word I just passed over the loud speaker?" He was excited and out of breath. The men all were.

Potts thought that this was a hell of a time for Rommel to be looking for compliments. The sailors didn't answer their division officer.

Although Popeye's battle station was in the upper part of the turret, right off the gun chamber, he went right on past it, climbing down the ladder to the gun pits, then on down to the shell deck and powder handling room below. It was what his division officer, Mr. Rommel, had ordered him to do.

Choosing to enter the turret another way, Norman Wiley, who was up on deck, ran back to the 4th division hatch. He jumped down the ladder to the living compartment on his way below to come up through the turret from the handling room to his battle station in the chamber on the center gun—a longer way but perhaps quicker as the crowd of running sailors swirled around him.

Acker, the cook, who had been standing nearby, saw the planes heading for the ship. "Boy, they ain't no shit in them apples," he said and jumped over the side.

Pinky Davenport, out in the boat, scrambled up the swaying Jacob's ladder to the boat boom, ran along it, and hit the main deck feeling like he was going about 110 miles per hour. It ran through his mind that he could have gone ashore, over to Ford Island, but the navy had trained him well. He would do his duty.

As Davenport ran across the deck, making for the 4th division hatch to go below, he saw torpedo planes heading in. The first torpedo was in the water, heading for the ship.

Down below in the living compartment, we had exploded into action as the call to battle stations and Rommel's words echoed in our minds. Frank Scott jumped up from his acey-deucey game in the rear of the compartment and looked out one of the portholes. Framed in the port, he could see a plane; it exploded as he looked at it. Francis Skifnes said, "I'd better get back to my ship." He left in a great hurry for the *Maryland* alongside.

Scott, shocked by what he had just seen out the port, ran forward to the ship's service compartment where the "gedunk stand" stood secured this morning, in order to go below and on up through the turret to his battle station in one of the upper powder hoist rooms.

Al Sandall couldn't believe the profanity he'd just heard over the general announcing system—the 1MC. From the very proper Mr. Rommel? He looked out a porthole and saw two torpedo planes coming in over the water toward the ship. He'd better get going. He could go topside, along the deck, and into the turret chamber to get to his battle station, or he could go down the hatch in the ship's service compartment, around the barbette through the carpenter shop, and down another ladder past the Lucky Bag and into the powder handling room, and then up through the turret that way.

Rommel had said bombs! He'd better go down, then up through the protective barbette if they were being bombed. That way he wouldn't be caught on the open deck. He took off, heading for the ladder going down. Rufus Nance ran along the same route to man his battle station.

Just at that moment, when we were rushing out of the compartment to our turret battle stations, Jack Miller saw the first plane drop its torpedo. He stared at the huge red circles on the wings as the plane pulled out of its run on the ship, skimming over the main top forward. Japs! They were Japs!

The gunners strafed the *Oklahoma* as the plane flew past. Jack swore he could see them grinning at him—just like in the movies. He moved fast to seek the protection of a large blower sticking up from the deck near the 4th division hatch.

Bob Roberts threw down his Sunday paper and jumped out of his bunk, heading forward to the next compartment to go down below along with most of the rest of us. It seemed to him that his feet were in motion even as he hit the deck and then it felt like he was doing forty knots as he ran forward. Like Sandall and Nance, he would go down and up through the turret instead of up and across the deck.

Three of the mess cooks—Shadow Bergstrom, Clarence Mullaley, and Dan Weissman—ran hard for the hatch, also heading below to the powder handling room. Moving as fast as I could, I ran in the same direction. Move! Move! Sailors were yelling, pushing in the excitement of the moment. Everything seemed a blur of action. Yet I was conscious of every step I made as I ran through the ship's service compartment, felt every rung on the ladder going down below. It was strange, almost as if it was in slow motion. But, of course, it wasn't.

Jim Stallings had just returned to the ship from an early morning motor-launch run and was down in the living compartment when the alarm was sounded. He took off with the rest of us, going below to the powder handling room where he had his battle station.

Red Templeton, sitting at the mess table, heard the general alarm, wondered what the hell they were having GQ on Sunday for. Then Rommel passed the word and he understood. He yelled for all hands in the living compartment to man their battle stations and ran forward toward the hatch to go below.

Back in the lamp locker, just aft of the 4th division head, Layton Banks was alone and still asleep when the attack began. No one will ever know what, if anything, he heard and saw during the last few minutes of life left to him.

The whitish bubbling wake of the torpedo pointed straight at the *Oklahoma's* port side, forward.

It was time for morning colors.

8

~~~

The torpedo slammed into the ship up forward. The Okie seemed to jump and a great shudder shook her, fore and aft. A tower of water rose high in the air to fall back over the polished decks.

I stumbled, but I was moving so fast, I stayed on my feet.

Miller saw it hit as the plane flew over the forward masthead. A second plane dropped its torpedo in the water. Miller hung on, yelling down the hatch to us below.

"It's the Japs, the frigging Japs! The shit's hit the fan!" I heard him yell and recognized his voice. It faded out behind me as I ran for my battle station.

The explosion of the torpedo shocked Arthur Claudmantle wide awake down in the blower space. He thought the boiler room had blown up. Big Ed Krames and Shanghai Walker woke with a start. The thud of the explosion following the call to general quarters had finally penetrated the fog of their sleep and they jumped to their feet. They looked out along the third deck passageway and saw black oil spurting up the sounding tubes from the fuel tanks down below. The force of the explosion had blown their caps off. Claudmantle still thought the boilers had gone; he and Krames dashed down the ladder to the handling room. Walker took off in another direction.

In the nearby MAA shack, the explosion threw the dominoes up in the air. Stanton Jones, wearing his brand new shoes, went down the ladder in the starboard trunk and into the handling room. Both Claudmantle and Jones had their battle stations in the upper part of the turret and would climb up through.

Mike Savarese was still in the living compartment when he felt the explosion. He put the tray of china bowls he was carrying to the scullery carefully on the deck. If they broke, he would have to pay for them, he thought.

Ordinarily, Mike would have gone topside and into the turret by way of the overhang. Not today; the ladder to topside was crowded with sailers coming down. He ran past a marine coming down the ladder. The marine yelled, "Here comes another one!" Mike ran forward to go down below.

Less than a minute had passed since the call to general quarters. No time to think. Just move.

The ship took on a slight list. Potts felt it up in the gun chamber, but only a few took notice of it—sailors topside with a view of what was going on. Down below we thought we were being bombed. "They're real bombs," Rommel had said. He'd said nothing of torpedoes in the water.

Seated in his pointer's seat in turret no. 4, Dick Whitman felt the ship shake. He had no idea what was happening. A hydraulic block? Did I cause trouble? I'll land in the brig, he thought. He looked around. Nothing . . . Everything seemed normal. Then he looked out the sight ports. The observation planes were sitting in their beds, the wings of one of them over the turret gun barrels. Usually, someone was sent outside to watch when the guns were trained or elevated—to make sure all was clear. Everything seemed okay outside. Whitman sat down in the pointer's seat and started up the elevation motors again.

Frank Scott couldn't get down the hatch in the ship's service compartment. He ran forward to go down another. He couldn't do that either; both were jammed with sailors crowding to get to their battle stations.

Scott ran aft, back through the two compartments, and started to go up through the 4th division hatch and into the turret from topside. Machine gun bullets rattled across the deck. He ducked back down and ran forward to the ship's service compartment again where he now found the hatch clear.

Down he went . . . into the carpenter shop. There were some sailors there, some sitting on a work bench that ran along the bulkhead. Just sitting there. Frank Wood was one. Scott thought he recognized Snuffy Arickx, too.

"It's war!" Scott shouted. "Why aren't you going to your battle stations in the handling room?" They just looked at him. "Wood, come on down where you belong!"

"I'm going to die," Wood said matter-of-factly. "If I am, it will be right here."

Scott was shaken by this, but he kept right on going, down the ladder in the trunk, on past the Lucky Bag, and into the powder handling room.

Cox'n Roberts was one of the first ones to get down the first ladder, around the barbette, and start down the ladder in the starboard trunk. Just as he hit the rungs of the ladder, the first torpedo hit.

The jolt threw him ten feet the rest of the way down, and he landed on his back on the bottom rung or the watertight door coaming. Perhaps both. Roberts couldn't move with the shock of it. Two men ran right over him and into the handling room. He knew he had to get up or be stomped right into the deck. He caught his breath back and managed to stagger inside the handling room to join some others already there.

Sandall was half way down the first ladder when he felt the explosion. He missed the steps to the bottom half and, traveling fast, he ran by the master-at-arms living quarters and into the carpenter shop.

Up in the turret chamber, Rommel felt the ship rock with the force of the explosion. What should he do? His battle station was up here, in the control booth where he could direct turret operations.

Instead, he started to go down through the turret to the shell deck, on the third deck below. The armored deck was the second deck down and the turret itself was heavily armored. The men would be better protected the farther down they went, he thought.

He did not tell all the men in the upper turret to go down with him, however, and they stayed put, manning their battle stations as they had been trained to do. They would be as safe here as anywhere else, safer probably.

Davenport, on deck, bounced down the ladder to be knocked off his feet as soon as he hit the living compartment. The volume of the record player jumped higher with the jolt of the torpedo hit, and the notes of "Let Me Off Uptown" sang loudly through the area. It was strange, Davenport thought. That's all he heard. Where was everyone?

Harold Johnson was in the living compartment when he felt the force of the hit. Water splashed down from the hatch above him. For some reason he thought it was mustard gas and he rubbed his arms as he ran forward and down the ladder, around the barbette, through the carpenter shop, heading for the ladder in the trunk going down to the powder handling room.

One after the other, most of us made it below and entered the turret. The time had never been faster.

Keep moving! Man your battle stations!

"This is no shit, God damn it! They're real bombs. This is no drill!" Rommel's words were still with me.

Red Templeton tried to go down the hatch in the ship's service compartment. He couldn't and ran forward to the hatch in the B division compartment. He was halfway down the hatch when the torpedo hit. The explosion knocked him off the ladder and he landed against the bunks in the shipfitters' compartment. They fell on him, but he wasn't hurt. He headed down and on into the turret.

The same for Nance, who, finding one hatch crowded, ran forward to the next, getting down to the shipfitters' compartment, then running aft to go into the turret.

Alone in the powder handling room when general quarters sounded, Clayton McQuay figured it would make a good air raid shelter—it was four decks down; the bombs would never reach it.

Now everybody was piling in through the door from the starboard trunk. Some of the sailors had their battle stations there and in the adjacent powder magazines. They stayed put, but others kept on going, climbing the ladder on up to the shell deck, into the gun pits, and finally into the turret gun chamber.

Everyone was excited but there was no panic. There was a lot of yelling and pushing as the turret crew scrambled to man their stations.

McQuay thought the ship was loaded with chinaware, the way it sounded. He could hear things rattling and breaking. He had felt the ship warp with the hit but it had only felt like a minor blow down there below the waterline.

No one could sink a battleship anyway, thought McQuay.

9

The second torpedo rammed into the port side, amidship, below the armored belt.

The *Oklahoma*, already hurt, staggered with the force of the blow. Lurching drunkenly, she took on a more pronounced list as water poured into the gaping holes in her side, flooding through the blisters and into the open spaces in the very heart of the ship. The flooding was rapid because the blisters and most other watertight compartments were wide open for Monday's inspection.

Water shot high into the air to fall back over her. Oil poured from the ruptured fuel tanks to spread over the harbor surface in an ever increasing semicircular wave.

The *Oklahoma* was mortally wounded. A great wrenching and groaning ran down her length as beams and stanchions, decks and bulkheads twisted and broke with the stresses put upon them.

As the reverberations of the explosions worked their way through the ship, there was a continuous crashing noise as the loose gear about the decks was thrown around—bunks, mess tables, dishes, lockers, everything. The single sounds seemed to blend into a huge cacophony of sound. Sailors caught in the direct force of the blast, or who were in the path of falling, breaking things, screamed as they were crushed to the deck, or looked at the water rushing in to engulf them were they lay.

Power went off and the lights went out.

Dick Whitman felt the ship shake again. What the hell is going on? The lights on the bulkhead were still on. Then the emergency siren went off in the turret. The control switch was in the turret officer's booth. Who had hit the switch? Why? Whitman knew that sailors would sometimes come into the turret, "light off" the switch, and take off just to aggravate the guys inside. Maybe I can catch the SOB who's been playing with the switch, Dick thought.

He ran up through the gun pits to the gun deck and into the booth. There was Ensign Rommel.

Rommel was yelling "The Japs, the Japs, the Japs are bombing us!"

Whitman asked the excited officer, "How do you know the Japs are bombing us?"

Rommel replied, "I just stuck my head out the hatch in officers' country and saw them bombing the *Helena* at 1010 dock and also dropping bombs on Ford Island."

The turret crew was coming up through the hatch into the turret.

Rommel said "Let's all go down to the shell deck where it's safe. And I'll send you up as replacements when the AA crews get killed. We can't fire the big guns in the harbor."

Jack Miller watched the second plane skim over the "fighting top," or mainmast. Like the first, the plane was strafing everything in sight. Miller picked himself up and ran forward for the break of the deck where a ladder led up to the 01 level, to do something—even if it was wrong. Someone on the *Maryland* alongside was firing at the planes. Our 5-inch 51s were in the casemates; they were broadside guns but they could fire straight out at the torpedo planes, at least. He wanted desperately to fire back.

The ammunition ready boxes were still locked. It was too late anyway. The decks were badly torn up. Jack ran down below to go into the turret and got to the shipfitters' shop on the third deck. The ship was listing badly to port. It was pitch dark—darker than hell, he thought. Work benches and equipment were sliding around. He got hold of a battle lantern so he could see where he was going and to keep from getting hit with sliding gear. A man was crushed right before his eyes. Who was it?

There was still some watertight integrity in the area, set by the sailors only a few moments before. Doors and hatches were closed and Miller couldn't make it any further to go into the turret. The rest of us had gone before. He'd have to go up again, up through the trunk to the main deck.

Clayton McQuay, in the turret, felt the ship jump and lurch with the second hit. The lights went out. The ship was listing. He climbed the ladder to the shell deck to check the shells secured to the bulkhead there.

There were more than 150 of the 1,400-pound shells standing against the shell deck bulkheads, secured in place by small stuff, or light line, only. They could break loose and break up the shell deck, maybe smash down into the powder handling room, thought McQuay. There was a hatchway between the two levels and it was open to allow the men to move up through the turret. When everyone had manned his battle station, the shell deck crew of Slapikas, Stapleton, Savage, and a few others would close this kind of trap door down, to lie flush with the shell deck. But for the moment, it was still open. It had nothing to do with the watertight integrity of the ship, or turret.

Deciding to stay where he was for the time being, instead of going up through the turret to his middle gun, McQuay looked around the handling room and saw four large drill projectiles secured to the starboard bulkhead, their 1,400 pounds straining at the light manila line that held them.

Davenport was right next to the record player up in the living compartment when the second torpedo hit. The music stopped abruptly. He thought the words "Let Me Off Uptown" were even a bit funny, considering the circumstances. He went down the ladder through the carpenter shop and saw Frank Scott. "Come on, let's go!" Scott shouted to him. Together, they dropped down the last ladder and into the turret handling room, among the last to arrive.

Al Sandall was running through the carpenter shop when the lights went out. He stopped to get his bearings. Sailors grabbed a couple of battle lanterns and he was able to get down the hatch and into the handling room. Quite a few of the turret crew were there already. He headed for the ladder at the powder hoist in the center of the handling room that led up to the shell deck.

I had bounced down the first ladder from the ship's service compartment, run around the barbette, and into the carpenter shop. When the torpedo hit—sounding much closer this time—the lights were knocked out by the explosion. I dared not stop, even though it was completely dark. I groped my way along and tumbled down the ladder in the trunk, slipping and sliding on the rungs, following the man in front of me, avoiding the feet of the sailor behind.

There was some light, just enough to see; someone had a battle lantern. I went past the Lucky Bag at the bottom of the ladder and through the hatch door into the turret handling room. I paused there a moment to catch my breath and wait for those ahead of me to start up the ladder at the powder hoist to the shell deck above.

Sailors gasped and swore with the urgency of manning battle stations. "Get moving! Move your ass! Get up there, damn it!"

Others . . . "Son of a bitch, what's happening? We're being hit!"

I had nothing to say for the moment. I started up the ladder at the powder hoist, climbing as fast as the sailor in front of me allowed. I couldn't tell who it was. The man behind was pushing at me and I didn't look around to see who that was, either. Still no time to think.

Mike Savarese was also in the carpenter shop when the lights went out. He made his way down the ladder in the starboard trunk. "Strike a match," someone said. "No, don't." A sailor did, anyway. Another had a cigarette lighter and flicked it on. Mike went through the door and into the handling room. Bob Lewis went in at the same time.

The auxiliary emergency lights came on and though the light seemed weaker, we could see okay. Everyone seemed to be inside now. Or should be. Close the door! Set Condition Zed to make us watertight.

We dogged down the watertight door to the handling room, striking down the metal fittings with a special dog hammer. There, it was closed. The handling room was watertight. Condition Zed was set.

Less than three minutes had elapsed since the call to battle stations.

Oil and hydraulic fluid from the training and elevation motors just above us dropped down on the steel deck of the handling room as the ship took on a list. Sailors milled around—those who had business in the handling room or had battle stations there—slipping and sliding, not knowing what to do. Some of us were climbing the ladder to the shell deck; others hung on to the powder hoist, still others grabbed at fixtures on the bulkhead to keep them steady.

Now the sailor in front of me was up; I grabbed the rung of the ladder as soon as his feet were clear. My head and shoulders were through the shell deck opening. The sailor behind me was almost climbing up my back.

I had to get to my battle station in the upper part of the turret—the starboard powder hoist room. Would I ever get there? This was my only objective at the moment. Seconds seemed like minutes.

One man was still missing of those who were still able to man their battle stations in the turret. He was the junior division officer, Ensign Joe Spitler.

10

~~

Red Templeton started up through the turret to his pointer's station in the gun pits. He moved fast and almost no one saw him on the way. Now Wimpy Hinsperger ran past him on the shell deck. Some others also passed him by, pausing briefly, as did Hinsperger, then moved on to man their battle stations. Bergstrom, Lewis, Savage, Slapikas.

Templeton was down on one knee, mumbling and fumbling with a shoelace. Sailors stopped, witness to this spectacle. Templeton was blubbering and shaking his head and saying something about what are we going to do, that he didn't want to die. Neither did anyone else, for that matter; most kept their heads and kept moving.

The men of the 4th division's turret no. 4 could hardly believe what they were seeing and hearing from the frightened boatswain's mate. They were sailors and they had battle stations to man! The young seamen looked at the broken Templeton, swore, and ran on. Tough guy, look at him. Jesus Christ!

Stanton Jones got up to his loading station on gun no. 1. On the way he had stopped on the shell deck to take off his brand new shoes. He didn't know why; it seemed the thing to do at that moment. When he got up to the gun chamber, there was no one there that he could see. Jones could feel the ship listing some. He decided to go below again.

Also moving up through the turret as fast as he could was Norman Wiley, climbing the ladders to man his battle station on the center gun, McQuay's.

Another who had managed to get up to his battle station in the gun pits, which Templeton had finally reached despite his difficulties on the shell deck, was his fellow boatswain's mate, Arthur Claudmantle. Claudmantle put on the phones but there was no answer from the control booth. He didn't see Templeton; it was dark. He heard someone say, it must have been Rommel, "All hands in the pits, seek cover on the shell deck." Taking off his phones, he headed back below.

Templeton stayed put where he was . . . for the moment.

Down on the shell deck, Claudmantle looked at the monstrous shells secured by what looked like six- or twelve-thread line. The ship was listing some. The emergency lights were on and he could see the danger all around him. I've got to get the hell out of here, he thought. No one in authority was there to tell him to do anything, so Claudmantle went down the ladder to the handling room below. Several sailors followed.

Ten-weight oil was all over the ladder and they slipped and slid on the rungs until finally they landed in the handling room. Claudmantle hung on to the powder hoist and put on the sound power phones. He tried to raise the booth again. No answer. Nothing. Somebody should be up there. But the turret officers were somewhere else—Rommel on his way down to the shell deck, Spitler not even in the turret yet.

"Go below. Go back down to the handling room!" Ensign Rommel arrived on the shell deck after coming down through the turret from the control booth.

I had just come up on the shell deck and I was surprised to see my division officer standing there in his dress whites. I looked at him, not understanding. What was he doing down on the shell deck? As the turret officer, his battle station was up in the control booth, I thought.

Ensign Rommel had not manned his battle station despite the call, "All hands, man your battle stations," a few minutes ago. There was no one in the control booth in communication with the rest of the ship or within the turret itself—as Claudmantle had just found out.

Every officer and man in the ship had been drilled and drilled to proceed to his battle station as quickly as possible, report it manned and ready, and stay there until ordered to secure or to abandon ship.

We were under attack.

My battle station too was up in the turret, not down in the handling room. I was determined to man it. Rommel had just said no. Perhaps he had a reason. What was it? What should I do? I stayed put for the moment, not knowing what to do.

Harold Johnson was down in the handling room. He was barely able to keep his feet with all the oil on the deck, and the ship was taking on a pronounced list, making matters worse. A few sailors had already slipped on the oily steel, lost their footing, and crashed into the port side bulkhead.

"What do you think of the Jap navy now?" he asked his friend who had sounded so confident a few days before. The sailor didn't reply.

Johnson saw a petty officer—Claudmantle—hanging on to the powder hoist and urging the men to man their battle stations in the handling room, trying to calm them down.

The emergency lights flickered. Two or three sailors were hollering and screaming to get out of there.

But there was no word up in the turret as to what to do. Claudmantle continued to try and raise someone on the phones. No luck.

Bob Roberts made it up as far as the shell deck, on his way up to the gun pits. Rommel said to go back down in the handling room; it was safer there. "And, besides, we can't fire the 14-inch guns, anyway," he said.

41

Rommel was standing near the same ladder he had just come down, trying to reassure us. We looked at him anxiously, quieting down so we could hear him plainly.

"Don't worry; she won't sink," he said. "It's safer down below in the handling room."

I wasn't sure of this, but I didn't question him in this emergency situation. He was the turret officer and I trusted him as did most of the others there. He must know best what to do, having been topside when the attack began, before coming into the turret. There wasn't time to think out our possible courses of action, anyway.

Rufus Nance had come up to join us and noticed that the shells around the barbette were sliding and bumping against each other. He saw Rommel and the rest of us clustered around him, heard the division officer say to abandon the shell deck. He watched some of the sailors start below to the handling room; but he continued his climb up to the turret chamber and his gun station.

Al Sandall also got up to the shell deck just in time to hear Rommel shouting, "Don't go any higher in the turret; we can't fire or train the guns." I looked around, saw the shells trembling against the bulkhead. I couldn't stay here much longer. Up or down?

Dick Whitman and Red Templeton were among the sailors on the shell deck. The emergency lights were still on, but the ship was taking on more of a list.

Templeton said to Rommel, "God damn it! The ship's going down. Let's get the hell out of here!"

Rommel replied, "No, they can't sink the ship with airplanes."

Red argued, "They can't sink the ship with airplanes? But they are sinking this SOB!"

"We'll probably have to go back to the States and get patched up," Rommel said.

Templeton was worked up and sounded off at his division officer. "You know you're supposed to be in charge. If anything happened to you, I'm senior petty officer here. Then I'd be in charge."

He continued, "And if you don't let us off here pretty soon, I'm going to knock you on your ass and then I'll be in charge!"

It was almost unbelievable. Templeton, the division bos'n's mate, challenging, then threatening Ensign Rommel, the turret officer. We looked on in disbelief.

Rommel took it. "Do you think the ship's going down, Red?"

"Hell, yes!"

Rommel said, "Let's go up to the turret officer's booth and see what's going on."

The ship was taking on a hard list. I realized it but did not fully appreciate the significance of this then. It was getting harder to keep your feet and we were grasping for something to hold on to. Rommel said, "Better clear the shell deck; those shells are going to start sliding around the deck and we'll get crushed if we stay here."

Rommel raised his voice again so everyone could hear. Our eyes touched briefly and I heard him say, "Stay here below the armored deck. Go down below. I'm going topside to see what's going on. I'll come back and let you know."

Following his orders, I went down the ladder. Roberts went down just before me; I was careful not to step on his hands. Others followed.

As soon as I hit the deck, I heard someone banging on the hatch door from the trunk to get in the turret. Sailors undogged the door and Ensign Spitler barged in, charged through us, and headed straight for the powder hoist, elbowing a sailor out of the way who was hanging on a rung of the ladder. He had almost run over me in his anxiety to escape the handling room. Frank Scott was another who saw him go. Spitler didn't say anything at all. His eyes were desperate; he hadn't even stopped to redog the door. Some sailors did it for him as he went rushing through us.

Where was his battle station? Up in the turret somewhere? In the booth? Maybe down here with us. I didn't know or care much just then. To hell with him. He obviously didn't care about those of us in the handling room.

There was considerable noise and confusion in the handling room as the ship, already mortally wounded, increased its list. Now everything that was not properly secured broke loose and went rolling and smashing along the slippery steel deck. Pandemonium reigned. Sailors were slipping and sliding around, some trying to gain access to the shell deck above. Several were trying to go up through the turret by the hand passage. The lights went out as they began to climb. The passage, meant to be used only in emergencies when the electric powder hoist went out, was just wide enough to pass up a 105-pound bag of powder, approximately the same diameter as a human body.

Seaman Second Class Jim Stallings and a friend, Seaman James A. Cuzzart, went for the hand passage. They were determined to work their way up through this narrow passage to the comparative safety of the upper turret and hopefully off the ship. Cuzzart had a pencil flashlight. A training shell broke loose and rolled down the deck.

Ensign Spitler spotted Stallings starting up the passage above him. He paused for a moment in his wild run through us. Spitler started yelling, "You're not going anywhere! You're at general quarters!"

Sailors looked at the raving officer. What's the matter with him, our eyes asked each other.

Spitler's head was at the same level as Stallings's feet as the sailor from Virginia started up the passage. Stallings kicked back with his foot and caught Spitler in the head. The officer was knocked off balance. Stallings and his buddy went on up the passage.

As Spitler scrambled up the ladder to the shell deck he met Sandall coming down the ladder on Rommel's orders and began hammering at Sandall's feet and legs. "Let me up! Let me up!" The pudgy officer screamed. He wasn't going to stay with the seamen in the handling room, for sure.

Sandall, faced with this assault from below, backed up on the shell deck. Spitler came up and started to wander aimlessly around. "What are we going to do? What are we going to do?"

The remaining sailors looked at him—Savage, Slapikas, Stapleton, some others as well as Sandall—and then at Rommel who said again to clear the shell deck and go below.

Spitler paid no attention and headed up through the turret. No one else had panicked on the shell deck—seaman or petty officer—except Templeton. So much for leadership.

Although his battle station was in the handling room, Johnson seeing Spitler run off and up the ladder, figured he had better get out too. He went right up the ladder, the second from the handling room crew to do so—not counting Spitler—just behind a sailor from California who had the same idea.

Lacking any orders to the contrary, the rest of us, twenty-five or more, stayed where we were.

As soon as Johnson reached the shell deck, he heard Rommel say, "Go back down!" The frightened sailor ignored the order and kept right on going, straight up through the turret as Ensign Spitler had done. He was right behind and went up fast. He had to get out of there! Never mind what Rommel had said. The Californian went right along with him. You couldn't blame them. Johnson didn't bump into anything at all on the way, he shot up so fast.

Now Rommel headed up the ladder to see what was happening, as he had said he would. Maybe he could help with damage control or something, he thought.

Dick Whitman followed. And Templeton.

Sandall now changed his mind about going below to the handling room and started up into the gun pits. His battle station was up there, anyway, on the ramming deck in the gun chamber.

The sailors that Rommel left behind him on the shell deck watched him leave. They would wait to see and hear what he would report to them when he returned. Then they'd know better what was happening and what to do.

Most of the men on the shell deck had gone below by now; a few had gone up through the turret. Some others, including Curly Slapikas, Doc Savage, and Kirby Stapleton, who were part of the shell deck crew, stayed where they were, manning their battle stations.

None of us down in the handling room believed the ship would sink, but some of us were beginning to wonder. We didn't have time to think. Everything that could move was breaking loose and crashing around. Excited talk and confusion mounted as we tried to figure out what was happening and what to do.

11

E nsign Rommel hurried up the ladders through the gun chamber and into the control booth where he had his battle station. He did not stay long.

He started out the hatch in the overhang of the turret to get out on deck. A blast of air from the third torpedo hit drove him back inside. It hadn't been more than ten seconds or so since the last hit, it seemed. A great gaping hole was torn in the port side, below the armored belt. More water flooded through the void spaces in the open blisters and into the broken compartments nearby.

Westley Potts felt the ship rock as if the main battery had fired. Should he go below like some of the others? He decided against it. The ship was listing well over, and he was worried she might go all the way.

Mike Savarese scrambled up the ladders in the turret to man his battle station in the gun chamber. He got into the pointer's pit, then up to the chamber, where he sat down to catch his breath. The explosion of the third hit shook the ship, and it seemed to Mike that she jumped out of the water with the force of the blow. Other sailors from down below were coming up to man their battle stations on the guns.

Rommel, back in the gun chamber now, shouted, "Everyone down below!"

Savarese didn't want to go back down to the dangers, known and unknown, of the shell deck and handling room, four decks below. Everything was breaking loose down there as the ship listed farther to port. Sailors were grabbing everything in sight to stay on their feet. The emergency lights were going. Besides, why should he go below? His battle station was here and they were as well protected in the turret chamber as anywhere else against the bombs that Rommel had mentioned. Better probably, with all that thickness of steel covering the turret housing—up to a foot of it.

Most of the sailors in the turret crew, except perhaps for Rommel and a few others, did not realize yet that the ship was being hit by torpedoes, not bombs. Most of us had been below when the action began.

"I don't want to go down," Mike told Rommel.

Rommel stubbornly said again, "Everyone down below!" They could hardly keep their feet. Savarese gave way. Rommel was an officer and he was only a seaman. Besides, he wasn't going to argue with Rommel's .45!

Faced with this double-barreled threat of officer and gun, implied or otherwise, there seemed only one choice to make. Back down to the handling room went Savarese. He had to climb down on a slant as the ladders tipped along with the ship.

Inside the upper port powder hoist room, Marion Athas and his friend could feel the torpedoes slam into the ship—feel it listing. They could see nothing nor were they told anything. They continued to man their stations.

Norman Wiley was up in the turret chamber, too, by this time. He had been knocked off his feet by one of the first torpedo hits on the way up. Now he saw Doc Savage, who had come up from the shell deck; Ed Beck (the gunner's mate), Red Templeton, and Rommel were there in the chamber.

Beck said, "Let's get out of here!" Wiley worried that an instrument used to measure the 14-inch gun riflings after firing, which was lashed down to the deck outside the turret, might break loose. He couldn't get it out of his mind.

Rommel said, "That's our AA going into action." Then, "Go back down," he deliberately told Wiley and the others there, trying to keep things calm.

The resourceful Beck told Wiley, "Stay put," so that Rommel couldn't hear him, and they backed up against one of the guns so he couldn't see them, either. What would happen next? Wiley looked at Rommel. It looked like he was wearing a pistol belt and holster, but why? They looked whitish in the artificial light. Where was the pistol?

Templeton made no move to go below as Rommel had ordered and said, like Rommel, "That's our AA going," whenever there was a hit or explosion outside. He looked pale and nervous.

Wiley was afraid Rommel and Templeton would see them hiding there. What would happen if they did? Would they make Beck and him go below? He didn't want to. It was terrible down there.

Some of the men were yelling and screaming, "What's happening? Why isn't someone doing something?"

Rommel continued trying to reassure the frightened sailors.

And the ship continued to list.

Frank Scott had come up through the barbette at the same time as Savarese. As soon as he got up in the turret, he saw Rommel and Templeton standing there in the gun chamber, near the control booth.

Rommel kept shouting, "Go back down!" He couldn't get the idea out of his head that everyone should go below although the ship was listing badly. Templeton didn't say anything.

Scott looked at Rommel and didn't move. He could see that Rommel had on a gun belt and a .45 pistol.

Scott looked around for a few minutes, trying to make up his mind what to do. It was hell down below; his battle station was up here. Then suddenly Templeton yelled angrily, "Get back down!" His face was deathly pale, his voice scared and excited.

Frank asked, "Why can't I stay here?"

"Because I told you to get the fuck back down, God damn it!" Templeton snarled.

Scott saw Templeton reach for a .45 pistol he was wearing at his side. Jesus, where did he get that, all of a sudden? He hadn't noticed it before.

Templeton repeated his order to Scott, "Get back down there like you were told, you son of a bitch, or I'll . . . " as he reached for the gun.

Scott didn't like the look in the boatswain's mate's eyes. He figured that Red would just as soon shoot him. Faced with this direct threat, Scott felt a wave of fear flood through his body.

Sailors who were close by and others who were climbing up behind the unfortunate Scott were witness to this confrontation in the turret. They couldn't believe what they were seeing and hearing. It was like a bad movie, Wimpy Hinsperger thought—in slow motion, it seemed, as each sailor reacted to this unexpected situation.

Where did Templeton get the gun? No one was allowed to have one in the turret. Or anywhere else in the ship unless specifically authorized. Only the officer of the deck and the quarterdeck watch carried side arms, and only when they were actually on watch.

What the hell was Templeton doing? No one said anything; they stared open-mouthed at Rommel and Templeton, not quite knowing what they should do. Their battle stations were up here, and they'd be safer up here too. The ship was listing more rapidly now.

Hinsperger and a few other sailors there knew what was happening. Only a few moments before, they had heard Rommel tell Templeton to see that everyone went back down in the turret as he had ordered them to do. Red now had a gun and confronted Scott while Rommel started off to take a look out of the turret. Perhaps he could help with damage control, he said. In a few moments, he was back. The ensign from Philadelphia tried to convince the sailors again, "She won't turn over or sink." He turned away.

Red Templeton looked hard at Scott and the rest of them, hand still poised over the butt of the .45. There was no question in Scott's mind that he was prepared to use it. He gave in to the division's leading deck petty officer.

"Go down, God damn it!"

Scott and some of the others turned and hollered back to the sailors coming up behind them to go back down below, and finally they began their long trip down, slowly, reluctantly, down into the hell and darkness. They stayed at different levels as they went, on the shell deck and in the powder handling room, three and four decks below. They had lost the contest of wills—backed by an authority they could not challenge—a .45 caliber pistol.

Scott and the others felt defeated, empty in some way as if all hope of escape and life was gone. No one said anything.

"Get goin'," Templeton yelled. Hinsperger and the others went below into the darkness of the broken, sinking ship.

One of those forced below from the gun chamber was my friend, the usually easygoing Doc Savage, scared and apprehensive now, the sailor who liked veal cutlets and pretty girls. He stopped on the shell deck to join Kirby Stapleton, Curly Slapikas, and a few others.

12

Pandemonium still reigned down in the powder handling room. Loose gear was sliding down the deck and crashing into the port bulkhead. Sailors were hanging onto the powder hoist and clinging onto the bulkheads. Some slipped and fell. Arthur Claudmantle fell and got up again. Clarence Mullaley fell on the slippery deck and someone reached down and pulled him up to the relative safety of the hoist—it looked like Savarese, but I couldn't be sure—and Mullaley hung on.

I grabbed for support where I was standing against the forward bulkhead. I saw the faces of my shipmates, frightened, anxious, unbelieving. As mine must be.

I'll have to watch those projectiles secured against the starboard bulkhead! They're going to break loose. They'll roll over and crush anyone in their paths.

Somebody tell us to do something! Near panic set in among the sailors there as they fought to save themselves and each other.

Schauf, Bergstrom, Weissman. Everett Gunning and Clayton McQuay. Lewis and Pinky Davenport. Roberts. Jupert Hall. We were all there. Dale Hamlin and some others.

Jones came in again from up in the turret; he didn't have any shoes on. Scott and Hinsperger dropped down from the shell deck above.

The emergency lights were still on, but growing weaker. The scene was indescribable, almost too much for me to comprehend. I could see and hear everything that was happening almost as if it were from some distance away. But I was part of the scene.

"They'll counterflood to starboard to correct the list," someone shouted. It sounded like Claudmantle. I repeated it to the sailors near me. Things seemed to calm down a bit. Most of us still thought we were being bombed, and felt relatively secure here in the turret, below the armored deck. We had not realized yet that torpedoes were tearing away the Okie's sides.

"My breakfast dishes must be breaking," I said to relieve the tension. I received a variety of replies, all profane. A few even laughed. The attempt at humor had its effect. For a moment, the voices and excitement died down.

Another hit! Closer this time.

The fourth torpedo hit the ship hard, above the armored belt this time because of the *Oklahoma's* heavy list to port. The ship rocked from side to side in her terrible agony. An almost inaudible moan sounded through the lower decks as the mighty Okie's vast insides absorbed the impact.

Men screamed and died.

Water poured into the stricken ship, from the great holes along her side and from up above, down through the openings in the deck and spaces overhead—ventilator shafts, access trunks, portholes, hatches— as the ship heeled well over on her port side. The water rose over the port side of the main deck as she listed. Masts and turret guns were leaning faster and faster to meet the harbor water . . . twenty degrees, thirty, forty, forty-five . . .

The roar of the water invading the ship drowned out the cries of the sailors as it reached out and engulfed them. There was no place to hide. None at all.

In the turret handling room, the men hung on for all they were worth, shocked by the horror of the situation. I clung to the bulkhead with my left hand, my legs spread wide against the list of the deck.

Water! Where was it coming from? I stared at the water spilling into the handling room, watched it rise along the lower end of the port bulkhead.

Where the hell was the water coming from? I felt the deck slip out from under me as the list grew worse.

A sailor lost his hold and slid down the oily deck to crash into the lower bulkhead. He lay there in the water, still. Another. I could do nothing. I held on desperately.

There was nothing any of us could do. Gear of all descriptions tumbled down the deck. Sailors scrambled and fought for the ladder going up to the shell deck. Should I try, too? I couldn't get across the deck to the hoist to even try.

It wasn't possible. The *Oklahoma* couldn't sink. What was going on outside? Why were we still down here? There was no word to abandon ship. Or any other word from the officers up in the turret. Nothing. Where was Mr. Rommel?

We better get the hell out of here. The thought came to most of us all at once; I could feel it and see it on the faces of the sailors with me. Someone was giving us an unheard order to try to save ourselves, that it was time to abandon ship. It was almost too late, anyway, for those of us who were trapped on the shelldeck and in the powder handling room.

Then, thirty seconds later, administering its coup de grâce, the fifth torpedo jarred ship and sailors again with a final explosion. We hung on. It hadn't been necessary. The ship was going fast. The lights flickered.

Meanwhile, Jack Miller was grasping his way up the starboard trunk space, alongside the barbette, trying to get topside. Oil and water cascaded over him as he walked up the bulkheads and popped out on deck. It seemed to take a lifetime.

And for many sailors in the 4th division and the ship this was true. The *Oklahoma* took on water rapidly. The flood progressed through all the open and damaged areas, forcing the huge ship to take on an ever-increasing list to port.

Up in the turret, Seaman Second Class Harold Johnson was one of the first out the overhang, right behind the sailor from California. Nothing could stop him in his effort to get out of that terrible place. The water was almost up to the centerline of the ship as he went out. As yet there had been no word to abandon ship. At least one other had gone out before them, however—Ensign Joe Spitler.

Spitler, who had ordered the sailors in the handling room to stay where they were, had abandoned his battle station to save his own life. Most of the men were still behind the turret. Some would not escape.

13

W ithout stopping except for those few moments on the shell deck, Spitler had gone up through the turret, on past the men of the turret crew whose sailors were manning, or trying to man, their battle stations, on through the gun chamber, into the control booth, and right on out the hatch in the overhang to hit the main deck beneath.

Almost no one had seen him go. He had nothing to say to any of the sailors he'd left behind as he made good his desperate attempt to escape the turret.

Ensign Joe Spitler from the state of Texas was one of the first, if not the first, men to abandon ship from turret no. 4.

Down below, in the handling room, Claudmantle was still trying to get someone on the phones up in the booth—Rommel, Spitler, Chief Turret Captain Brown, anyone—to ask for instructions. But no one was on the phones. What should they do, he thought. There was still no word to do anything, not since Rommel had ordered everyone below. Nothing on abandon ship. Nothing at all.

Out on deck, the frightened Spitler grabbed hold of a hatch cover so he wouldn't slip down the deck and into the water. It was beginning to come up over the port side as the rails dipped under.

Johnson, the seaman second, saw him there as soon as he came out of the turret overhang, and he hung on to his junior division's officer's legs so he wouldn't slide down the deck himself and into the water. For a big man, Spitler had got out fast, it occurred to Johnson. He himself had come up through the barbette so fast it seemed that he had hardly touched the rungs of the ladder. And here was Spitler, out ahead of him.

There was still no word to abandon ship, either by phone or by passing the word by voice down through the turret. Most of the men were manning their battle stations or seeking protection, as ordered, on the shell deck and in the powder handling room. A few were still trying to climb the slanting ladders to their battle stations up through the barbette. Still others were already in the upper powder hoist rooms, on the loading platforms, and in the gun pits.

Everywhere through the turret, most of the sailors of the 4th division were doing what they had been trained to do, as best they could. All of us were scared, but we didn't have time to think about it much. Some of the 4th division sailors were already dead.

Only a few minutes had passed since the call to general quarters . . . frantic, action-packed moments of eternity.

In the upper part of the turret, Rommel, Westley Potts, and several of the men gathered around the hatch in the overhang. They waited there a few moments; the list was getting worse. They looked at each other, then down at the hatch. It was a way out. Not quite yet, though.

Rommel bent down and started to close the hatch. Potts said better leave it open as they might have to get out. Then Rommel opened it all the way and looked down at the main deck, a few feet below. Potts told him he better step back or a bomb blast from outside might get them. So Rommel closed the hatch a little and they waited there, around the hatch, their only means of escape from the turret.

But not for long.

Rommel looked out the hatch again and saw water coming across the deck. So did Whitman. Rommel said, "You men stay here and I'll go outside to see what's going on."

He went out the hatch. His feet were in the water coming over the deck. He hollered, "I believe the ship is going down. Tell everybody to get out. Make sure you use the voice tubes; make sure everybody gets the word; make sure they get the word in the lower handling room."

A few may have heard him. Whitman did. "OK, OK."

And Rommel was gone.

Then, all of a sudden, Red Templeton was there and he went out. Right along with Rommel. Where the hell had he come from?

Aghast, Potts and the others in the control booth watched them go, the first ones out, leaving the rest of the turret crew—more than forty men—behind. Potts didn't see the trio of Spitler, Johnson, and the Californian depart.

Still no official word to abandon ship. No word to abandon ship got down through the turret to most of us. No word, either, to those down through the barbette to come up to the relative safety of the upper turret.

A few moments before, Red Templeton had come up out of the gun pits, through the chamber, and into the control booth. Except for those brief moments when he and Rommel had confronted the seamen in the turret crew and forced them down below, the leading boatswain's mate of the 4th division had been on his own.

There had been the confrontation with Rommel on the shell deck. He'd threatened to knock the division officer on his ass. Rommel had caved in, but he had smartened up and now they could get the hell out of there.

All kinds of loose gear began to rattle and bang around in the pits— lockers, trash cans, bright work polish cans, and the like. Oil spilling down from the guns above began to slick up the deck and the ladder going up to the loading platform in the gun chamber. It was dark. A bit of light filtered in from the open hatch in the overhang. Templeton could hear others in the pits with him, but he couldn't see who they were. He thought he heard them going up the ladder and out of the pits, leaving him alone.

Could it be Claudmantle, the sightsetter; Roberts, the firing pointer; Oleson, the trainer . . . who?

One was Whitman. They had opened the hatch to the gun pits on the way up from the shell deck. Dick, too, was sliding around as the oil slicked everything down. He made it up to the turret officer's booth.

Red figured maybe they were glad to leave him here alone, the bastards, he thought. Templeton cursed and swore as he fumbled around, trying to keep his balance. Sons of bitches, letting him tumble around with all the trash by himself, he thought. Who are they? Well, fuck 'em all, whoever they are, Red said to himself. Templeton couldn't get a grip on the oily ladder. He was desperate, here in the dark and all alone. Goddamn ladder! He thought he heard someone yell to abandon ship. He had to get out of here! He was finally able to get his footing and go up the ladder.

Claudmantle, for one, had gone down in the turret again on Rommel's orders, not up. Roberts never made it. It could have been Oleson that Red thought was leaving him behind. Or Whitman . . . If so, they hardly qualified for the verbal abuse Red had heaped upon his unknown companions.

When Templeton finally arrived in the control booth, he saw only one man besides Rommel standing there, Oley Oleson. In his mind, he did not or would not notice the other sailors who were still in the booth and gun chamber. He did know that most of the turret crew was still below. Whitman saw him running around, beating with his fists on the unused port hatch. Red was desperate. Then Rommel had gone out.

And there in the gun booth it was Oleson and Templeton for the moment. Red said, "Everyone's gone; let's hit it." It wasn't true. Potts was right there, Dick Whitman, too. Edgar Beck and Wiley pushed back against the gun so Rommel and Red couldn't see them and send them below.

"No, you go," Oleson replied.

The two first class petty officers looked at each other, then out the hatch in the overhang where they could see water coming over the deck. They could save their lives perhaps by abandoning the turret. An uncertain future awaited them inside the ship—sure death, Templeton figured.

Oleson said again, "You go. I'm going to wait a few minutes. I have something to do."

"I'll see you," Red said and dropped out on deck and into the water. The ship was listing about forty-five degrees when he went out.

Rufus Nance went out about this time, just after Red.

With Rommel and Templeton out of the way and gone apparently, at least from the gun chamber, Ed Beck made his move from where he was backed up against the gun. "Abandon ship!" he screamed. Wiley was just ahead of him and Beck was behind Wiley, pushing and yelling, "Let's go!" Wiley saw a couple of men go out of the turret ahead of them. Who were they? He couldn't tell.

The two sailors ran up from their hiding place and through the control booth. "Abandon ship!" Beck was saying, "Let's go!" He was still yelling and pushing Wiley along.

Rommel and Templeton couldn't keep them there now, they thought. The ship was going over, sinking. Jesus, let's get out of here.

Why did they tell them to go below? All those guys down there. Spitler didn't count; he was long gone, anyway. Oleson was still inside but he was an okay guy, he wouldn't stop them. Now . . . let's go. And they were out!

Wiley thought he saw Templeton hanging on to the side of the ship as she listed. He slipped down the deck into the port side lifeline and broke his arm. Yes, it looked as if Red were still there, just below the blister. He must have been one of the two he saw go out ahead of him, the seaman thought. His arm hurt.

Oleson wanted to jump. But he couldn't do it. There were all those men inside. They were friends, shipmates. McQuay was there, he was sure. He couldn't abandon them like that. It just wasn't in him. He'd rather go down with the ship than not try to warn them somehow.

Besides, he couldn't swim, anyway, so what the hell? The decision was not an easy one but he made it. The little turret captain went back inside the gun chamber to do what he had to do.

During this time, unknown to us in turret no. 4, the same kind of drama was unfolding up forward in our sister turret, no. 1, and also in turret no. 2, just aft of no. 1. The official order to abandon ship had come from the second in command, Commander Jesse Kenworthy, the executive officer after the torpedo hit, because Captain Bode was ashore.

Ensign Francis G. Flaherty, US Naval Reserve, the assistant 1st division officer and no. 1 turret officer, heard the order to abandon ship. Realizing the lives of his men were in great danger, he shined the beam of his flashlight around the darkened turret so they could see to escape.

In no. 1 turret, Seaman First Class James R. Ward, a member of the Okie's baseball team, also heard the word to abandon ship. He knew his shipmates would be trapped in the turret as the ship turned over, so he too shined light down through the turret so the men could come up from below and go out the hatch in the overhang.

The two men, officer and seaman, hung on desperately, remaining behind as the turret crews abandoned, assisting and urging on the sailors remaining so they would not die, trapped in a sinking ship.

Back aft, Ensign Rommel swam away from the listing ship as fast as he could. He looked back just once, saw the ship he'd just abandoned halfway over, no. 4 turret going under, her guns pointing in the air.

Rommel turned away from the terrible nightmare of the ship in her final torment. Like Lot in the Bible, he thought to himself, he would not look back again lest he be consumed. He could not help them now . . . the young sailors of the *Oklahoma*'s 4th division and turret no. 4 . . . his men. It was too late.

Red Templeton looked up at the capsizing ship, his home for the past nine years—home to hundreds of men he knew. The huge tripod masts were closer to the water now. "Gee, that looks funny," he said to himself.

Spotting Rommel in the water, Templeton let go his hold of the ship and swam over to his division officer. Rommel was still in full uniform and was hanging on to the oily grating of the division's accommodation ladder, which was floating in the water.

Templeton laughed out loud with relief at being safely out of the turret and off the ship. He said nothing of the sailors inside the turret that had been left behind.

Nor did Ensign Rommel, who just looked at him and said, "We've got to get away from the ship; the boilers might blow up."

There was fire on the water, and the two men pushed away from the sinking *Oklahoma,* through the oil and debris. They could no longer hear the screams of the sailors inside the turret.

Templeton was still laughing. Rommel did not look back. The bright gold ensign's stripes on his uniform shoulder boards were already tarnished.

The division officer wished he had told his men to abandon ship. It would haunt him the rest of his life.

PART 3

Abandon Ship

14

"Abandon ship! Abandon ship!"
The fateful word that all sailors dread echoed down through the turret.

McQuay told us in the handling room to be quiet so we could hear.

It was Oleson who was yelling down the turret. McQuay would know that voice anywhere. "Abandon ship!" They better get out of there fast, thought McQuay.

Mike Saverese recognized Oleson's voice, too.

The awful reality to abandon chilled those of us who heard the word passed down to the handling room. Many didn't hear it, in the individual struggle for survival. It was difficult to hear and absorb everything that was going on around us. I heard several voices say to abandon ship but couldn't recognize who they belonged to in the confusion of the moment.

Marion Athas, confined in the tiny powder hoist room, off the gun chamber, had felt the ship buck and jump with every torpedo hit. What should he do?

It was all happening so fast. Athas stayed there, imprisoned in his small room. It was his battle station and that was where he was supposed to be. He could see nothing, nor could he hear what was going on. The ship listed sharply and he hung on.

Then suddenly, Oleson stuck his head in from the gun chamber and yelled, "Abandon ship!"

Athas scrambled out of the hoist room and out of the turret. So did the sailor with him. Slipping down the deck outside, Athas got his foot caught in the deck winch. He couldn't free himself. The ship kept going over. He'd be caught here and go under with her! Athas frantically tried to get free. He called for someone to help him. The water was coming up over the frightened sailor.

Down in the gun pits, Al Sandall also heard the word to abandon ship. Sandall yelled down through the turret to the others below, "Abandon ship!"

Sandall slipped down the deck with the list of the ship, banging into the outside of the turret. But he managed to get up the ladder to the loading platform in the gun chamber, run around the range finder, then drop out of the turret. The water was close to the hatch as he went out the overhang. Grabbing anything in sight, Sandall climbed around the outside of the turret.

Westley Potts saw a couple of big emergency power batteries lying there on the deck of the control booth, and it looked as if they were going to fall on him as the ship kept turning.

"Do you think those batteries will fall on us?" he asked the sailor beside him, Gunner's Mate Dick Whitman. "Ah, no," he told Potts; they're all right."

Just as Potts was going out the overhang hatch, one of the batteries broke loose and tumbled down, hitting him in the chest and stomach. Urged on by the battery, Potts fell the rest of the way out of the turret, slid down the deck, and into the water. Whitman came out right after him. As far as Potts could tell, he and Whitman were the last two men to leave the upper part of the turret.

Everett Gunning, hanging on to the powder hoist in the handling room, heard the word to abandon ship and went straight up the turret ladders. The emergency lights were going and the ship was listing so far over, it seemed he was climbing sideways. Somehow, he made it up to the gun chamber and the booth. He tried to go out through the overhang, but the hatch was jammed. Gunning went out the narrow shell ejection hatch on the bottom port side of the turret.

He saw several sailors hanging on to the high side of the deck. Japanese planes were strafing the ship. A chief petty officer yelled, "The ship is going to turn over!" Gunning leaned against the gun turret on the highest part as the water came up to his feet.

Sandall saw Athas with his foot caught in the winch and could see that he was going under as the water came up over the deck. Athas was calling for someone to help him. Sandall's first reaction was to keep right on going and get off this sinking ship. But, because he was the kind of man he was, he had second thoughts and managed to get over to Athas and help him get loose.

Athas looked up and saw another familiar face, turret captain Harald Oleson. He was working to free Athas as the ship increased its list.

Oleson had got everyone out of the upper turret. He had indeed something to do, as he had told Red Templeton. The men below he could not help any more than he'd done by yelling down to them to abandon ship, lest he go down with them, too. Oley went out the overhang of the turret and slid down the deck . . . one of the last, if not the last, to make it out of the turret by that exit.

Oleson couldn't swim, but he didn't have time to think of that minor matter at the moment. When Athas was free of the winch, Oleson helped him hold onto a hatch for a minute or so until they could catch their breath. The grateful Athas figured the turret captain had saved his life. He and Sandall.

In the powder handling room, Pinky Davenport made a last try for the hatch going up to the shell deck. Five or six sailors were in front of him, all trying to get up and out as death closed in on them. They were yelling and hollering, "We're going to be killed!" A petty officer, Roberts, who shortly afterwards got hold of himself, was screaming and crying, "I don't want to die."

Jupert Hall cried out in despair, "I can't swim!" Davenport looked at him and swore in disgust.

I didn't have anything enlightening to say at all for the moment, so I didn't say anything. I was too busy trying to stay upright, hanging on to the forward bulkhead, in any case.

Water poured into the lower part of the handling room faster and faster as the ship listed. Terrified, we watched the water rise. We were trapped.

Davenport came back down the ladder. "Get back up there!" Saverese yelled as Davenport backed down on him. Mike shoved up at him, his hand on Davenport's rear end.

"I hear shells breaking loose up there," Davenport replied. They got no farther. He got a faceful of blue dye as it spilled out of one of the projectiles just above him.*

The blue dye spilled down over Frank Scott, too. He also heard the projectiles breaking loose, rumbling down over the slanting deck, to crash into the interior port side of the barbette.

I couldn't get over to the ladder on the hoist in the middle of the handling room. It was too far to reach without letting go where I was. The deck was at too much of an angle; it was slick with oil. I tightened my hold on the bulkhead; I was barely able to stand.

I looked up toward the shell deck. I could only guess what was happening up there. But I think I knew down deep. I could not acknowledge it yet.

I looked at the water flooding into the handling room. It was rising up the deck toward me. A sailor, arms and legs afly, slid down the slippery deck in front of me. I couldn't see who it was, and he splashed into the water and lay there. Another went down the deck on the other side of the hoist. His scream was cut short when he hit.

Stanton Jones could hear the smashing and breaking sounds above as the shells broke loose and tumbled down the deck.

At that point, no one could get up the ladder to the shell deck. The huge 1,400-pound projectiles had broken loose from their lashings. The sailors trapped there could do nothing to save themselves. The last thing they ever saw was dozens of 14-inch common and armor-piercing projec-

---

*Various colored dyes were used for ship and gun identification to spot the fall of shot. When the projectile exploded, a colored spray of water could easily be seen and corrections made in range and bearing.

tiles rolling down the deck at them. Their screams ended abruptly as they were crushed into the deck.

A collective sigh seemed to come from the sailors in the handling room as each pair of eyes looked up to see what they could hear but not see. Our shipmates were crushed to death, we knew. How many, we didn't know.

Among those killed on the shell deck were my friends Lyal Jackson Savage, Kirby Stapleton, and Edward Slapikas.

15

"**S**he's going over!" A sailor said to Scott where they were hanging on the powder hoist. They said good-bye to each other.

Scott's clothes were saturated with oil and dye and water. He felt a chilling cold come over him. His ears hurt as the air pressure increased in the handling room.

With the possibility of escape up through the shell deck closed to him, Dale Hamlin tried to make it up through the hand passage in the powder hoist. He could barely squeeze his way up the narrow passage meant only for the emergency passing of the 105-pound powder bags.

I watched him make his try, wriggling and squirming until he disappeared, but I didn't think he could make it. Possibly, but not likely. I certainly wasn't going to get hung up in there. There must be another way.

Shadow Bergstrom tried next to get up the hand passage, as Hamlin had. Had Hamlin made it up? He didn't see him up ahead. Bergstrom struggled desperately to work himself up through the narrow confines of the passage. He was having a hard time of it, even though his body was thin. Pieces of metal inside the passage clutched at him, trying to imprison him there.

But the two seamen who had been threatened by Spitler, Stallings and Cuzzart, had managed to squirm and squeeze their way up just before Hamlin and Bergstrom. It was tight going. Thank heaven for the pencil flashlight. The ship continued to list. They made it into a temporarily watertight space in the upper part of the turret. The ship was rolling; the turret was going under water.

Stallings and Cuzzart kept their heads and figured it out. They would open the hatch. There would be a flood of water, but they would go out against it and swim away from the ship and up to the harbor surface.

That's what they did. They had to swim hard. The oil on the water was on fire.

"Abandon ship!" again. Some heard; some didn't; and some acted while others didn't, or couldn't right then.

Just at that moment, it became apparent to several sailors that the only way out of the handling room now was through the same hatch door and starboard trunk by which we'd come in. There was a rush to the starboard side of the handling room.

"Get the Goddamn door open!" someone yelled. "We've got to get out of here!"

But the ship was going over. The door was quickly getting out of reach as it rose above our heads with the listing of the ship.

Frantically, sailors near the door reached for the metal "dogs" that would release the door. They had been banged down tight after we had come into the turret and set Condition Zed, to be opened and closed again when Spitler made his entrance and exit. Now no one could find the mallet that could hit the dogs back up so they could unlatch the door.

"Where's that frigging dog hammer?" a sailor yelled. "Son of a bitch!" another swore in frustration. Sailors beat on the dogs with their bare hands, not feeling the pain.

Then in desperation, Roberts, swinging like a monkey, climbed up to the door, which was nearly overhead by now. He tried to hit the dogs loose with one hand while chinning himself with the other. I wished I could help him, but there was no way I could.

The only man in the division who could chin himself with one hand. Who would ever think that it might help to save his life some day? His own and others. Now all the dogs were loose except one or two. Roberts lost his hand hold and crashed down on the listing deck and into the water.

"AAAh!" A scream cut short.

Roberts was not alone in trying to get the door open. In all the excitement, Arthur Claudmantle had not heard the word to abandon ship, but he was one of the men at the door trying to get it open. Another one was McQuay, who had got the word.

From my vantage point diagonally across the handling room, it looked as though they would never get the door undogged and open. The rugged Stanton Jones hung on with one hand, prying and hitting at the dogs. "The frigging things are stuck!" a sailor yelled. I dared not let go my grip on the bulkhead for fear I would lose my footing.

The scene in the handling room was wild: sailors clustered around the powder hoist, frustrated at their attempts to get up the ladder to the shell deck; those who were frantically trying to get the trunk door open;

others, slipping, sliding, hanging on as best they could—all of us trying to keep our feet as the deck listed under us more and more. A few lay motionless in the water that continued to flood up the deck to the living, seeking us out.

Finally, the door swung open. It hung there, swaying a little. Sailors latched it still. "Jesus Christ," someone implored to an unseen presence. "Let's get out of here!"

Jones went out and right up the trunk, climbing the ladder fast. He'd make it out if he could; he was moving sideways, almost horizontally now, with the list of the ship. He had to keep moving! There! He was all the way up and out of the escape hatch on the main deck. One out.

McQuay began to climb up the trunk. Four decks to go. The ship was listing badly. He made it up. The hatch on deck was only a few feet above the water when he came out. McQuay splashed into the oily mess. Someone or something pushed him down, down again. He was exhausted. But he had made it so far.

Even now Bob Lewis didn't believe the ship was sinking, even though water was pouring down through the trunk into the lower handling room. He hadn't heard the word to abandon ship either, but like the others, had decided to get out of there. Lewis even thought he'd find another battle station somewhere else where it was not so dangerous. He helped the sailors at the door to get it open.

Lewis saw some men go up the trunk, ahead of him. Thinking he was the last out of the handling room, for each man was almost totally preoccupied with himself and his immediate and total effort to survive to have anything but an impression of what was going on around him, he got up the trunk and came out the escape hatch by turret no. 4. Stepping on the barbette, Lewis slipped off into the water. She was about to go over. He'd have to get away from here when she went or he'd get sucked back into the ship.

He was the third one out.

The ship was so far over now that Arthur Claudmantle was getting hit with the water coming down the darkened trunk. He felt two or three men run over him in the dark and confusion. None of them had time or hands for battle lanterns. They were running right up his back, pushing him under water, jerking him off the door.

"Son of a bitch," he gasped, "get off me." The emergency lights glowed dimly behind him, in the handling room.

The easygoing Claudmantle got mad. He just had to get out. He fought his way up the trunk, could see some light coming down from topside. The ship was listing and going over. He went up along the trunk as fast as he could.

The *Oklahoma* was almost lying on her side. Water was flooding in. The force of it knocked him around. He had to get out of there!

Coming back down into the handling room from his futile attempt at escape up the powder hand passage, Bergstrom saw that the men had gotten the trunk door open. But no one was around that he could see. Where was everyone? Had they all gone?

He made a leap for the ladder, which was swinging free in the trunk. Water was coming down. He tried to climb the ladder. "God help me!"

Like Lewis, "the Shadow" thought he was the last man out of the handling room. Actually, there were more than a dozen of us still there, around the powder hoist, and hanging on the bulkheads. A few were still trying to get up the ladder to the shell deck. It seemed hopeless, but they had to try.

Bergstrom was the last to leave the handling room by the trunk.

The water poured down and over him. He was tumbled around by the force of it. Choking, gasping for air, the young seaman fought to survive the terrible twisting and turning. He couldn't see. Or even call out. His mind was slipping into oblivion and it was dark.

While this group of sailors was fighting to get the trunk door open and make their escape, the rest of us in the handling room were making our own fight for survival.

After Roberts had fallen into the water, he had managed to regain his feet and grab onto the powder hoist. Mike Savarese was there, and so was Scott. Davenport, too. Popeye Schauf, Dan Weissman, Wimpy Hinsperger, and Clarence Mullaley. I was hanging on across the deck from them. All of us were struggling to stay on our feet and not go crashing down the deck into the water and debris.

I had heard the projectiles let go on the shell deck just above me. I guessed what had happened to the sailors there. Now, looking at the drill projectiles secured against the upper, starboard side of the handling room, I became acutely aware of the danger. These huge shells would come smashing down at us at any time. The emergency lights were still working, and we could see.

I had to do something, I knew. But the deck was so slippery from the oil and slanting so much, I couldn't get over to either the door (which they were trying to open, and finally did), or to the powder hoist, without releasing my hold on the bulkhead. The powder hoist was just too far to reach and if I let go, I'd slip down the deck and it would be all over.

I kept my head; I had no choice. I looked quickly at the projectiles straining at the line that held them. It would not hold them much longer. I would be crushed to death if I stayed where I was.

There was only one thing to do.

"Catch me, Bob; I'm coming across!" I shouted across to Roberts on the hoist. I saw Roberts and Savarese reach out for me. "Come on, jump!" they yelled.

I jumped away from the bulkhead, leaping across the space between us, just as the shell above me broke loose to rumble down over the deck where I had been a moment before. I was in midair, committed; my life was in the hands of the men on the hoist.

There! Someone—it was Roberts—grabbed my wrist and arm and my weight swung me down across the deck. Just don't let go.

I looked up and there was good old Savarese along with Roberts. One man alone couldn't pull me up, but the two of them managed it. Savarese had my arm now. The two of them pulled me up to the relative safety of the hoist. "Thanks," I said.

We were temporarily exhausted from the effort and hung on to each other and the hoist. I looked up to the shell deck. Was it too late to try to get out that way? Could it be done? I'd have to try or I'd be down here forever. Savarese hung on; he could hear the water gurgling into the turret.

The emergency lights went out! The darkness was absolute.

Roberts tried to get up the ladder in the hoist. I came up behind him. Roberts thought as I did, that this was now the only way out. We heard the shells rolling around the shell deck over us. We couldn't see; it was pitch dark.

Roberts groped his way up to the opening that led to the training motors and found the hatch to the shell deck closed. It seemed hopeless but he had to try. Bob pushed up through the narrow space filled with the motors. The listing of the ship made it that much harder.

Was it all over for us, there in the turret? Like Roberts, I couldn't accept it. Not yet.

There was a man in front of him and Roberts was pushing hard at him from behind. We just had to open that hatch to the shell deck. It was the only way. Someone was pushing me from behind. We couldn't open the hatch. Jesus Christ! The shells must have jammed it shut.

It was too late for the sailors left in the powder handling room of turret no. 4. We were trapped. There was no way out!

16

Up on the main deck, aft, Marion Athas was finally successful in climbing up on the side of the turret. It had been a close call. Thank heaven Sandall and Oleson had got him free of the winch.

The *Oklahoma* was practically on her side. Athas stood on the side of the turret; he looked forward to turret no. 3 and saw Hutch Wortham trying to cut a life raft loose.

The no. 2 turret officer, Ensign Norman C. Hoffman, made it out and went over the side.

Roy Stewart, turret captain in no. 2, got out and walked up the bottom. He didn't even get dirty.

Sandall watched a sailor from the 3d division slashing away with a fire ax at the lines that secured another life raft to no. 4 turret. Al climbed up on the side of the turret and tried to help him. The lines were covered with paint and he couldn't untie them. Finally, they chopped the raft loose and slid it into the water. The ship was almost over.

Standing on the side of no. 1 saluting gun, Sandall jumped. He grabbed the raft and discovered that one end of it was caught under the muzzles of no. 3's guns. The guns could take the raft down with the ship as she rolled over. Al let go his grip on the life raft and started to swim for a seaplane floating upside down in the water nearby. It was the *Oklahoma*'s, the one that had been on the 4th division's catapult.

When Dick Whitman dropped out of the turret to the slanting deck, he managed to grab a hatch as he went out. There was a mushroom blower on the side. A sailor was hanging on the blower. "Stick your leg down here and give me a hand," Whitman called. He got hold of the sailor's leg and swung over to the barbette.

The ship was leaning way over. Whitman looked at the life rafts. They were tied down and he hollered for something to cut the lines. Dick slid down the deck in a curve as the ship rolled under him. A sailor grabbed him at the life lines. They used a fire ax to chop the lines loose on the balsa life rafts. There were two rafts and two groups of men, ten or twelve each, managed to get hold of them. The water was coming up fast.

Whitman was in the water. He swam, head down, to get away from the ship. It looked like the ship was going to roll over on them. Sailors were covered with black oil; Whitman too. He grabbed onto a water breaker floating by, for support.

"Goddamn it, Whitman, get your own water breaker." It was Chief

M. M. Brown and he had possession of it. Whitman got hold of another and the two were able to find enough support to keep their chins above water.

An older chief was in the water. "Good-bye, good-bye. I'm drowning!" he cried.

Brown and Whitman grabbed him and hauled him up over the water breakers. A passing motor launch saved him.

They looked up in the sky and saw three low-level Japanese planes in formation. They dropped their bombs and the sailors in the water ducked. The bombs hit the *Arizona* and she went up. There was fire in the water. Puffs of smoke from the antiaircraft fire covered the sky overhead.

Rufus Nance tried to climb up on the starboard side of the turret too, but the angle of the deck was too steep. He couldn't do it. He went into the water and saw a sea sled, used to recover the observation planes, secured to the side of the no. 3 turret.* A sailor yelled, "Let's cut the sled off!"

Nance and some others cut it loose so they could use the sled as a life raft. They shoved away from the ship. More sailors jumped off the side of turret 3 onto the sea sled and it went under with their weight. Some of the men let loose and began swimming out into the harbor, away from the ship.

The large boatswain's mate stayed where he was—on the sled. He noticed that the splint and bandage were gone from his broken finger. "Gawd damn! I'll lose the finger for sure now," Nance thought.

A bomb hit the *West Virginia* just aft of the stricken *Oklahoma.* Harold Johnson let go of Ensign Spitler's legs and hit the water. Spitler was still hanging on the hatch. Johnson swam toward the Okie's seaplane floating in the water.

Norman Wiley began to swim away from the ship as fast as his broken arm would let him. When he surfaced for air, he was only a few feet away from the ship. A passing motor whaleboat hit him and broke his leg.

A sailor grabbed Wiley and pulled him up on the side of the ship. With his good arm he hung on to the lines that secured the *Oklahoma* to the *Maryland,* inboard.

The Okie's executive officer, Commander Jesse Kenworthy, immaculate in his dress whites, walked up the side and onto the bottom of the listing ship. Wiley watched him do it. A big red-haired sailor he didn't

*In normal conditions a *sea sled* was put over the side from the fantail and allowed to trail in the water a hundred yards or so astern. The ship turned as the seaplane descended for a landing, in order to create a patch of smooth water for the plane to land on. A deck winch pulled the plane in after it had hooked on to the sled, and the aviation crane on the fantail hoisted it aboard.

know jerked Wiley's good arm from the line, and he almost went under before he could get back to it.

Everett Gunning dived in and swam away from the ship under water. He surfaced for air and saw the starboard rail coming over at him. Swimming away again, Gunning surfaced and got to the floating plane a few feet away.

Westley Potts, in the water, figured he better get out of there before the *Oklahoma* went all the way over . . . the suction might pull him under.

Clayton McQuay was almost done in when he came to the surface from out of the trunk leading down to the handling room. He got to the seaplane and hung on there with the other men. The plane was starting to fill and was settling in the water. "You look just like Al Jolson," he told a sailor whose face was covered with oil. The sailors in the water were all trying to get hold of something—anything—to support them in the oily water.

Potts noticed a second seaplane, the one from the no. 3 turret catapult, floating nearby, right side up.

Chief Brown said to Dick Whitman, "Well, beaver-puss, we won't have to shine any more bright work today."

Ensign Rommel and Boatswain's Mate First Class Templeton were well away from the ship by now, moving out into the harbor.

Overhead, the battle raged. The sky was full of enemy planes; bombs fell to explode on ships' decks and in the harbor water. Bodies and bits of bodies clothed in liberty dress whites and the uniform of the day flew in the air. Machine guns stitched along the ships, the bullets indiscriminate in what they hit—gunners, men going over the side, the wounded, and the dead. Torpedoes slammed into the great warships along Battleship Row. There was fire in the sky and oil upon the water. The smoke from burning ships blocked out the sun.

The Okie sailors who were abandoning ship or already in the water were, to a large degree, unaware of the destruction being done in the harbor by the attacking Japanese aircraft; they were intent on their own individual efforts to escape the sinking ship and . . . to save themselves. What concerned them most was that particular area in which they lived for the moment—a few square feet of ship or water.

But in less than ten minutes, the Pacific Fleet had been put out of action, smashed and immobilized by an insignificant enemy out of the Far East, from the land of the rising sun.

Suddenly, the *Oklahoma* rolled over, port side ripped open by five torpedoes and flooded with tons of water. Her great tripod masts dug into the mud bottom forty feet down. Supported by her masts and superstructure, her lower starboard side and bottom remained a few feet above the water. She looked like a stranded whale. There was a great bubbling and frothing around the capsized ship as the air belched and burped from her torn insides.

In turret no. 1 Ensign Flaherty and Seaman Ward remained at their stations despite the order to abandon ship, continuing to hold their flashlights so the rest of the turret crew could see to escape. Ignoring the chance to save their own lives, these brave men stayed at their posts to the very end, their flashlights beams of hope until the ship made her final plunge and the water rushed in to snuff out the light.

The mightly *Oklahoma* had capsized; her great gaping wounds poured fuel oil from deep within to spread in ever-widening circles over the harbor surface.

It had taken less than ten minutes for this proud ship to die; exactly eight minutes after the first torpedo hit. In less than twenty, her massive weight of thirty-five thousand tons had settled heavily into the mud, her death throes done. She had rolled through 150 degrees and had come to rest at a 30-degree angle from the vertical.

The Okie took more than four hundred sailors—officers and enlisted men—with her. Some died during those first terror-filled moments, others took longer as they frantically sought to escape the water that engulfed them.

Among those lost was the Catholic chaplain, Lieutenant (junior grade) Schmitt. He died a credit to his calling. Trapped at his battle station on the second deck below when the ship went over, Father Schmitt helped several sailors escape through a porthole to safety. When he in turn tried to squeeze through, he was unable to do so, quite possibly because of the breviary in his pocket. Then, seeing that other sailors had entered the rapidly flooding compartment for a means of escape, Chaplain Schmitt insisted he be pushed back inside to assist them. True to his commitments as a priest and a naval officer, he urged them on, helping them to safety out of the porthole before the water engulfed him there.

It was over. Done.

The *Oklahoma* was no more.

"All hands, keep silence about the decks." Taps for 20 officers and 395 enlisted men.*

Two-thirds of her crew would survive and most would go to sea again in other ships, but navy life would never be quite the same again for any of the sailors who had called the battleship *Oklahoma* home.

*Total casualties: 448.

70

17

~

S tanton Jones watched John Wortham go down with the ship. There was nothing he or anyone else could do to save him and Hutch drowned, despite the rooster and pig tattoos on his feet. Mary, his wife, never knew about the missing finger.

Marion Athas was still hanging on to the ship when she rolled over. He jumped into the water and started swimming toward the seaplane. There was so much oil on the water he could hardly breathe. He hung on.

Close by, a young sailor said "So long!" and just let go. He disappeared under the water. Athas and the others couldn't help him; it was all each man could do to keep himself afloat.

Arthur Claudmantle was thrown back in the water as the ship went over. He was caught under the deck, fouled up! "Red Devils" danced before his eyes. He held his breath and tried desperately to get out from under. Finally, he came up where the gangway had been and got tangled up in the lifelines. Art was on the verge of passing out. He couldn't go on. He had to, that's all! The water was muddy, slimy. And finally there was sunlight. He'd made it.

When Art had left his Connecticut home to enlist in the navy his mother had asked him not to get tattooed or married without letting her know. He got the tattoo and hadn't let her know.

And there was a pretty little Mexican-American girl named Mary back in Long Beach . . .

Rufus Nance looked around and saw the seaplane from no. 3 turret. A sailor was swimming toward it. He watched the man climb up out of the water and into the cockpit. What was he doing? It looked like he was trying to start the plane! The sailor looked around the cockpit as if he was ready to fly the plane away at any moment. Transfixed, Nance watched this bit of drama unfolding before his eyes. He thought he recognized one of the 4th division boatswain's mates, but he couldn't be sure. Then, apparently unsuccessful in whatever he was trying to do, the man climbed out of the cockpit and went back into the water. Nance was mystified.

The sailor in the plane was one of the 4th division petty officers, Westley Potts, who had spotted the plane, swam to it, and climbed aboard. He tried to untie the knots that secured a canvas cover over the two cockpits. The knots were oily and Potts couldn't untie them, so he ripped off the cover and climbed into the front cockpit, where the pilot ordinarily sat. It was the first time he had ever been in a plane.

In the excitement of the moment, with roaring enemy planes and explosions of all descriptions inspiring and urging him on, Wes had an idea he might be able to start the plane and taxi out into the channel, away from Battleship Row. But, how to do this?

Looking around the cockpit, Potts pushed and pulled everything he could find. In the back of his mind he seemed to remember something about the pilot being able to fire off a shotgun powder charge to turn over the propeller. Still no luck. It didn't occur to him at the moment to think how he would be able to stop the plane, even if he did get it moving.

Frustrated, Potts climbed back into the rear cockpit, where the radio-man-gunner sat, looking for a machine gun to fire back at the Japanese planes diving down at the ships and sailors in the harbor. The machine gun wasn't there; it had been removed.

Potts could see the Okie going over and he jumped out of the plane back into the water, swimming furiously to get away from the ship, toward some pieces of wood floating nearby. Just as he reached the debris, the *Oklahoma* went all the way over, taking the plane he'd just left with her. Men were in the water everywhere. Potts knew that many of his shipmates, including the crew of turret no. 4, had been trapped and gone down with the ship. He held on to the pieces of wood, his mind numbed by what he saw and felt.

Norman Wiley pulled himself up on the bottom of the ship. The broken bones in his arm and leg hurt like hell. His face hurt too, for some reason.

Claudmantle looked at Commander Jesse Kenworthy standing on the bottom in his whites, dressed for inspection, Art thought.

Then, Claudmantle spotted what he thought was a lifeboat upside down in the water. It was partially covered with water and looked like a small whale, at first glance, he thought. It was the sea sled from no. 3 turret. Rufus Nance was lying on it. Claudmantle decided that Nance looked more like a walrus than a whale.

Nance lifted his hand. "My finger," he said sorrowfully. Fire was spreading around them.

"Let's get out of here," Claudmantle said.

Nance said, "I'm staying here; my finger's hanging off." He showed it to Art.

"Can I help you? asked Claudmantle in the water.

"No."

"I'm sorry, I'm getting out of here," Art said, swimming off. Nance was still stretched out on the bottom of the sea sled with his finger dangling over the water. Claudmantle watched the Japanese dive-bombers make their runs over the ships in the harbor. He was glad he had learned how to swim back in Long Island Sound when he was growing up.

Nance looked back at the capsized ship. There was Smokey Keenum, the chief master-at-arms that Rommel didn't like, standing on the bottom. He must have walked around the hull as she turned over.

Inside, Shadow Bergstrom was thrown back and off the ladder as the water engulfed him from above. Above? Below? The words meant nothing as the *Oklahoma* capsized.

Bergstrom fought to hang on, to grab something—anything. The force of the water spun him over and over. He couldn't see. There was only the noise of the water as the Okie drowned. He was going down with her, he knew. Was this the end of him?

Suddenly, it was over. He had stopped spinning. He was in the water and . . . over there! There was light! The light was coming from some portholes . . . just enough light to see that they were the large twenty-four-inch ones. By their size, he knew that somehow he had wound up in chief petty officers' quarters, on the second deck, starboard side, just above the carpenter shop.*

The water was rising fast. Bergstrom followed the water up the slanting compartment, grasping for things to hold on to. He was walking up the overhead, in fact.

When the compartment fills, there will still be some air in here, Bergie thought. He knew that from somewhere. The water continued to flood in. He was in a corner in the high side of the compartment. Everything was quiet. Water was flowing in through the portholes. He was under water, inside the ship, but enough light was filtering down from the surface to outline the ports.

The only sounds he heard were mysterious tappings echoing here and there in the ship around him. His shoes were off and he wondered how he'd lost them.

Bergstrom hollered out. A voice answered him! The two sailors called back and forth in the darkness and finally located each other.

The other man was Quartermaster John Gercevic.

Gercevic had heard the alarm where he was asleep in steering aft, five decks down. Taking the time to pull on his trousers, he had managed to make it up the ladders as far as the second deck, despite the explosions caused by the torpedoes ripping away the side of the ship. He had no idea what was happening; he was on his way to his battle station on the bridge.

The ship rolled over as Gercevic ran along the listing deck. He could

---

*The starboard escape trunk went straight to topside from down by the turret no. 4 handling room and Lucky Bag on the first platform deck, up to the carpenter shop on the third deck, then chiefs' quarters, and out on the main deck.

see light coming from the starboard portholes, which were now to port, on the low side of the compartment, and headed for them. Water was flooding in as the ship completed her roll.

Desperately, he tried to make it out of the porthole, but the incoming water was too much for him, and the force of it pushed him back inside the ship, spinning and tossing him around and around.

"My God, I'm drowning!" John thought. And, suddenly it was quiet. The Okie had capsized.

Trapped in steering aft was fellow quartermaster Al Ellis, who hated to stand quarterdeck watches with Ensign Rommel.

Was Gercevic alone in here? It was too dark to see. There was air but he'd suffocate eventually, unless he could get out, he said to himself. But how? For just a moment, John panicked, banging his head against the steel of the bulkhead. Let's get it over with, he thought. His head hurt and he stopped. He was thinking clearly again.

John called out and a voice—Bergstrom's—replied.

The two were so relieved to find each other that, despite their predicament, they enthusiastically cheered on the gunfire they could hear outside the ship as U.S. gunners fired back at the attacking Japanese aircraft. Hope for survival was renewed.

Bergstrom felt around for the now submerged portholes with his feet. He felt the dogs on the sides, measuring the width with his legs spread wide.

"Do you feel it?" he asked Gercevic.

"Yes."

The two of them decided to dive down and try to get through and out of the ship. They were lucky that the portholes were not dogged shut as they should have been at general quarters.

Bergstrom dived down and managed to get through. It was a good thing he was on the skinny side, he thought.

He went up through the water and broke the surface. They were still under attack. Bergstrom saw the broken lines that had secured the *Oklahoma* to the *Maryland*. They were covered with oil. He tried to climb up the side of the ship, but his hands kept slipping. Finally, he made it and stretched out on the bottom for a time, exhausted.

Gercevic was now alone. Had Bergstrom made it? John waited; Bergstrom didn't return. Was he drowning? Dead? Gercevic felt something brush against him and he grabbed at it. It was a foot! The foot of a dead sailor floating in the water. Gercevic recoiled and let go fast.

Now it was time for him to go . . . to make that all-out effort to get out of the ship through the porthole and save himself. He took a deep breath and ducked under water.

There! He was through and rising toward the surface. His chest hurt and lights danced before his eyes. Then, suddenly, his head broke the surface of the water and he was back in the world again. Gercevic grabbed hold of a line hanging over the bottom of the ship. For the moment, he was safe.

Bob Lewis was actually out of the ship when she turned. The turbulence in the water caused by the Okie's thirty-five thousand tons was too much for Bob. The force of the water swept him back down the hatch opening he had just come out of.

Lewis grabbed the edge of the hatch and held on to the coaming with all his strength. He mustn't be sucked back inside! His fingers were almost wrenched from his hands as he fought the water. He let go.

Lewis was swept back inside the ship. The force of the water banged him around, tearing at his body and rolling him around, scraping the skin off his shoulders, face, and head.

Was this the end?

Suddenly, the water stopped pushing him around. Now it was rushing in the portholes, just like the intakes in a drydock when it was being flooded, he thought. Men were clawing at each other, fighting to get out.

Even then, Lewis didn't realize the ship had sunk; it just couldn't happen to a battleship. As the compartment filled with water, Lewis knew he was going to drown. He said good-bye to his mother and started to swallow water to get it over with as fast as possible. He felt a gloriously happy feeling come over him and slipped away into unconsciousness.

Then he came to. Someone pulled him up by the hair of his head and into an air pocket. It was Alvin Brown, the sailor he didn't get along with. Brown had felt Lewis's body brush by his legs and yanked him up. Two other men were there, one of them named Whitey. Lewis had come back to life—for the time being, anyway. He could breathe. The four of them had their heads up against the overhead, which only a few minutes before had been the deck.

The deck? Then they realized the position they were in. The ship had turned over—capsized. The overhead was below them! The water in the compartment was about shoulder level high. They could just feel the portholes with their feet.

Lewis inhaled deeply, ducked under the water, and got his head and one shoulder through the port. The other three pushed at him to get him out. More skin was torn off his shoulder. It was too painful; the port was too small, no more than 14 inches in diameter. He knew he couldn't get through. The other three were larger than he was, and if he couldn't, they couldn't.

They heard air bubbling in the water to one side of them. Were they losing it or gaining it? There was a hatchway there leading into another compartment. Which one was it? They had no idea.

The four went in, anyway. There were big overstuffed mattresses floating around. Then they knew they were in chiefs' quarters. Using their feet again, they discovered portholes. They were the large-sized ones—twenty-four inches in diameter. They could get through!

But the four sailors were skeptical about trying; they might swim into the mass of another ship, get blocked, trapped there in the water outside.

Gercevic and Bergstrom had done it earlier, but they didn't know this.

Brown suggested to Lewis that since he had pulled Lewis out of the water into the air pocket, Lewis should make the first try and come back to let the other three know what the score was.

Lewis noticed by this time that they were holding their noses against the deck which was now the overhead. A few minutes ago, the tops of their heads had been touching the deck overhead and the water had been chin high. The air was going. They had to act. Lewis agreed to go first.

He inhaled, dived under the water and out the porthole. Swimming hard, he was exhausted with the effort. On top of that, he didn't know what direction he was swimming in. Up? Down? He quit trying to swim. He felt his body rise through the water. Then he was at the surface and out.

What a sight! There was a motor launch over there picking up survivors. But they didn't see him! No boats were near him that he could see. Then a sailor of one of the boats spotted him and they came full tilt to the rescue.

"There're three men trapped in the air pocket down there," Bob told them.

One of the sailors in the boat immediately discarded his life jacket and dived into the water to go after them. Just then Brown, Whitey, and the other one of the three popped to the surface and they were hauled aboard.

Jim Stallings and his buddy were picked up out of the fire and water by a captain's gig and taken to safety on Ford Island. They were happy to be out of it.

18

Those of us who were left behind down in the powder handling room during those final seconds when the ship capsized were not aware at first that she was turning turtle. The darkness there was wild and confusing with objects of all descriptions being tumbled and thrown about. As we frantically fought to save ourselves, we became disoriented. It all happened so quickly that we could hardly grasp what was going on.

During those few short minutes, the officers and men had been put to one of the greatest tests they would ever know. For those of us trapped in the sunken ship, our fight for survival had just begun.

Roberts had been on the shell deck ladder when the Okie rolled over. Someone had said, "Here's an opening, let's go." He scrambled up. But it wasn't up. It was down! There was a lot of noise. And it was dark.

How did this happen? thought Roberts. These battlewagons are unsinkable.

The door to the trunk fell off. The brass cotter keys that held the hinge pins in place were routinely polished and had been for Monday's inspection. The man who had this job didn't put the keys back in so that he could lift the hinge pins free to polish them too. Because the cotter keys were out, the pins had nothing to hold them in place, and the door just fell off. It was kind of funny, considering all the effort some of us had put in trying to open that door.

I felt the ship lurch. The deck slipped out from under me and my hands snatched at empty air. I was tossed and spun around, pitched into a great nothingness, suspended in air as the ship turned about me. It was as if we were in a suspended state of animation for the few seconds that all of us—the living, dying, and the dead—were whirled around together, bodies pointing in all directions.

Quickly the water flooded in. We were buffeted about, twisted and turned by its strength.

Then the dark waters closed over me as the ship came to rest—upside down on the bottom of the harbor.

I surfaced, gulped for air, and automatically began to swim, or more exactly to tread water, in the confining space of the handling room. I was surprised to find myself alive.

Frank Scott wondered if he was still alive. He could hear voices. He scrambled and walked over the overhead and bulkheads, knocking his shins against various pieces of metal. They hurt like hell. He was cold as hell. He must still be living, he figured.

Pinky Davenport was thrown back off the ladder as I had been, and found his head stuck between two pipes. He tried to pull them apart with his hands. Look out for the shells, he thought. Water threw him against a bulkhead.

Mike Savarese heard the roar of the water as it came into the handling room. Then it was over. Everything was quiet.

I heard Popeye Schauf call out, "I can't swim! So long, guys. I can't swim!" His voice echoed through the steel darkness of the handling room.

Savarese said, "Take my leg." His arm was wrapped around the powder hoist.

I swam over to Popeye and grabbed whatever hair he had and helped him to stay afloat.

Over there! Someone had a light. One of the emergency battle lanterns.* It was eerie, there in the blackness, the white light reflecting from the glistening steel bulkheads and the smooth black water.

"Here. Over here," a voice said. The light moved toward the opening to the starboard trunk.

The handling room was half full of water. We must be in an air pocket, I thought, the water seemed to have stopped coming in. Saverese and I helped Schauf over to the trunk space and momentary safety.

Seeing the light like a beacon in the absolute blackness of the handling room, the other surviving sailors there followed it to the trunk space—Mullaley, Weissman, Davenport, Hinsperger, a few others.

Two or three bodies floated quietly in the water behind us. We left them there in the handling room where they had died.

Now, everyone who could make it was in the trunk. Roberts was there. Howard Aldridge, the balding red-haired boatswain's mate first class from the 4th division who was also the Okie's postmaster, was there. So were a few men from the powder magazine that supplied the turret.†

Some sat on the ladder in the trunk. I stretched out on a narrow metal overhang; Hinsperger was next to me. Both ladder and overhang kept us out of the water, at least for the time being.

"Well, what do we do now?" I asked Wimpy. He had no suggestions. We tried to orient ourselves. The ship was upside down, that we knew by now. There was no panic now that it was done. What could we do? How

---

*All turrets in the ship were equipped with a number of powerful portable battle lanterns for use in emergencies.

†Besides the 4th division sailors mentioned in the text were the following: Seldon Goins, a seaman first who had two brothers in the ship and who was sometimes called "Comin' and Goins"; Seaman Second Class Garlen W. Eslick; Rogers R. Tillman, an electrician's mate second class; and John R. Engen, a musician first class.

could we get out? Survive? Was there a way? Or were we hopelessly trapped in the bowels of the ship on the bottom of Pearl Harbor?

Time passed; it was hard to say how long. Each man thought his own thoughts. There was a little talk and Aldridge, the Texan, said, "Don't talk, you'll use up the air." He was the senior man present of the fifteen or sixteen who were there in the trunk. We used the light sparingly while we collected our thoughts. "Turn it out," from Aldridge again. "Don't use up the batteries." We would need it.

After a little, I said, "We didn't even fire the guns, Wimp." "Yeah; it don't matter now."

The *Oklahoma* had just gone through its annual short-range battle practice when the ship's four gun turrets had fired for record. A year ago, in 1940, the 4th division's turret no. 4, containing three monstrous 14-inch guns, had worn the navy's *E* and three hash marks painted on its sides for four successive years of first-place shooting. Then suddenly no. 4 lost it, and the coveted *E* for excellence and the hash marks had been painted out. This year, the turret crew had tried hard to regain this recognition by constant drill, day and night, but had failed again. I was part of it now and was as disappointed as the rest. I had been surprised to feel only a sort of thud inside the turret when the guns let go a salvo. Almost no noise at all. But we had worked well together and there was always next year. I was impressed at the smooth and intricate manner in which this great gun turret functioned. We were a team and even though the turret was an instrument of war, it was good to be part of it.

Perhaps this disappointment was a sign of things to come. The Okie had been a good ship for duty since her commissioning twenty-five years ago just before the United States' involvement in the first World War. Although she'd served on North Atlantic patrols and on convoy duty during that conflict, her guns had never fired in combat. She had survived the war and enjoyed the peace that followed.

And now, perhaps, she was showing a few signs of old age, which affects machinery and men alike. There had been that business with the broken propeller shaft a few months ago, in August. The *Oklahoma* had been on her way back to Long Beach for a bit of leave and recreation when we'd run into an unusually heavy Pacific storm. The buffeting about the huge thirty-five-thousand-ton ship had received had broken her starboard shaft, and we had to go into Hunter's Point Shipyard in San Francisco for repairs. Not that anyone in the crew seemed to mind this diversion from Long Beach—it was still the States—but maybe the stresses and strains of long service were beginning to set in.

Then there was this thing with the *Arizona* a few weeks ago when the Okie had returned to Hawaii and Pearl Harbor. There had been an exercise at sea, and one dark and squally night the two great battleships had committed the unpardonable sin of colliding with each other. Actually, there had been little damage done; for the ships had managed to turn in time to avoid a smashing impact. Each had received a glancing blow as their sides had brushed. Nevertheless, it had happened. The collision alarm had frightened everyone, particularly when we thought about what might have been. We'd been lucky. Even now a board of inquiry was meeting to determine just how this could have happened.

A second near miss around the same time had come when the *Oklahoma* and the fleet carrier *Enterprise* had somehow gotten on a collision course. Over the PA: "Collision forward" . . . "collision amidship" . . . "collision aft!" Then the "All Clear." We had just barely averted disaster, the Big E's bulk twisted over the Okie's flag staff on the stern, it was so close.

Just over a year ago, the *Oklahoma* had made the Seattle papers in a rather bizarre incident that involved the collision of the huge battlewagon with a string of barges carrying railroad freight cars across the sound.

The *Oklahoma* had not really been at fault; she had gone out of the Puget Sound Navy Yard in Bremerton on a short trial run when it happened. There was patchy fog in the area; the tug that was towing the barges sounded fog signals at regular intervals. When the tug broke out of the fog, she stopped her signals, although the freight cars on the barges remained obscured. The *Oklahoma*, also in the fog, thought the danger past, when there out of the mist appeared the silhouette of a freight train! It was a strange sight, indeed, to Quartermaster Gerald "Dutch" Foreman and the others on the Okie's bridge. The ship banged into the string of barges, scattering them and damaging a couple of freight cars. It was a good thing there was little way on and she was moving slowly. The papers had a field day with their headlines, and the Okie sailors took a lot of razzing in town from sailors off other ships.

19

B ob Roberts was thinking. He had to do something to help the guys and himself too. If he ducked under the water in the lower part of the trunk, would he be able to find his way down to the next level and up into another area which might offer a way out? The shipfitters' shop was up one deck. Or one deck down now. "I'll come back and let you guys know," he said, taking the light.

Where had I heard that one before? He would if he could, I guessed.

"It's a good thing we've got Eveready batteries in that battle latern," I observed. No one said anything.

Davenport was thinking the same way as Roberts. If they could make it up—or down—under the water and try to find a way out through another compartment, then maybe they could make it out. But, maybe the other spaces were full of water. There was air here in the trunk; it was dry, except for the lower part. But for how long? We were trapped. We had to find a way out of here.

Come back if there's a way out, Pinky," we said. "Okay. Come on, Scott," he said, and, taking a deep breath, he left. Scott stayed in the trunk.

Savarese had to try too. Promising to return, he ducked under water and tucked his hand up the other side. The water level was the same. He found himself in the shipfitters' compartment on the third deck. But with the ship over, he and the others were actually deeper down in the ship. It didn't matter; it might offer a way out.

Savarese smelled something gassy. He recognized the area—there was all the machinery. He swam forward to the other end of the compartment. There must have been twenty or thirty sailors there. The men from the trunk flashed their light around. There was the conveyor belt. He asked the sailors, "Is there a way out?"

"No."

Savarese said his prayers for about the third time.

There was some talk. "Two guys went to the other end of the shop. There's a hatch there."

"Is there any way out?"

"They went out and they didn't come back."

"What happened?"

"We don't know."

Savarese went aft toward the carpenter shop and saw two sailors in a small corner of the compartment. They were just sitting there. He said his prayers the fourth time.

Frank Wood was one of the sailors. He said, "I'm twenty-nine; I've lived my life."

Savarese told him, "What the hell's the matter with you? I'm only nineteen and I'm looking for a way out."

Someone said, "Let's go." But Wood stayed behind. It was his choice and they swam off.

Mattresses and bedding floated in the water. They pushed against some bodies and the lifeless sailors bobbed off along the water. The deck was overhead and the overhead below.

Then Davenport saw Wood there in the carpenter shop. "What's the matter?"

Wood told him, "I lived my life. It was a tough one and I quit." The words shocked Davenport. He would remember them always, would see Wood's face before him as long as he lived.

But what could he do?

Davenport swam forward and looked around the shipfitters' shop, saw the conveyor belt upside down, and continued moving through the compartment. It was difficult to see his way along. There had been a second light at first but someone had dropped it in the last compartment when he recoiled from a dead sailor he'd bumped into. Now they couldn't find it down in the water. The one light was all they had now.

Davenport, like Savarese, headed back to the trunk. There was no way out of here.

Roberts had first worked his way through the shipfitters' shop. He saw a blond-haired chief petty officer and a couple of sailors banging away with a dog wrench at a big navy lock on a store-room door, trying to get in.

Even if they could get the door open, it didn't lead anywhere. But maybe they could get closer to the outer hull where they could bang on it and he heard from the outside.

They got the lock off but couldn't open the door. It was jammed from the inside.

There was little to be gained by staying there. Roberts thought maybe he should go aft and swim underwater to the steering room aft, which would be close to the outer hull. He didn't know then that there were seven men imprisoned in the steering room. Al Ellis was one.

One of the sailors started to pray and said he was going to stay where he was. Roberts figured maybe he wanted to stay with the chief in the shipfitters' shop. In any case, Roberts didn't feel he had the right to try and convince him that his (Robert's) way of dying—trying to find a way out—was the best. It was the sailor's choice to make.

Bob headed back for the trunk space along with Savarese and Davenport. Bunks and debris, the bodies of the dead floated there in the still water. A hand stuck out of the water in silent supplication.

There! Someone's head. Savarese grabbed at it. The head moved . . . back into the trunk. They followed.

"There's no way out," Roberts said.

"It don't look so good," Savarese said.

"Shit," from Davenport.

"We're trapped," I said hopelessly, looking down at them from my perch on the overhang a few feet above.

Roberts didn't say anything. He turned off the light. It was dark again.

I laid back down on my steel bed, my eyes open, looking into the darkness. "Remember San Francisco, Wimp?" I asked Hinsperger who was stretched out next to me. "We had some good times there."

"Yeah."

We had enjoyed our stay in San Francisco early that fall. The cable cars, Joe DiMaggio's restaurant on Fisherman's Wharf, the Oakland Bay Bridge, and Telegraph Hill. We wandered around Chinatown and the International Settlement, enjoying it all, even the notorious Brass Rail down on Mission Street where Templeton got socked by the big boatswain's mate that night. The better dance halls and ballrooms gave forth with the music of Woody Herman and other popular swing bands.

Wimpy Hinsperger and I went to see the University of California play football in Berkeley and Santa Clara right in town. And Ray Vidito and I walked the streets and up the hills, sightseeing. Even the fog that rolled in from the sea each afternoon did not dampen our spirits. Its glistening, slippery wetness reflected the colored lights of the city as the Okie sailors saw the sights, frolicked and played, went to the movies or to bed.

Eventually, her bottom cleaned and painted, her starboard shaft repaired, the *Oklahoma* received orders to get under way and rejoin the fleet at Pearl Harbor. The sea detail was set, the anchor hauled aboard, and the 4th division sailors brought in and secured the port boat boom, aft, and the after accommodation ladder, sometimes called the gangway. The watch was shifted from the quarterdeck to the bridge. All boilers were put on the line; the great engines waited for the engine order telegraph on the bridge to signal "Slow Ahead."

The men in the 4th division stood at quarters on the port side of the main deck, aft, wearing their undress blues. The current ran strong in the bay and it was salty cold as we got under way. I looked around the bay at San Francisco and over to Oakland, then up, as slowly the *Oklahoma* moved out of the harbor, under the Golden Gate Bridge, and into the vast Pacific, her bow pointing toward the Hawaiian Islands.

I shivered a little as she plunged into the first heavy seas outside the bay. Salt spray flung up over the forecastle stung the sailors there, whipping aft along the weather decks as the bow dug deep into the cold water. The cold wind from far to the north lifted the collars of our jumpers and flattened out trousers against our legs. Thrown off balance by the heavy seas, we pushed hard against the wooden deck, our feet wide apart in an effort to regain our sea legs, unused these past few weeks.

The *Oklahoma* was old, but she had a kind of dignity with her broad beam and tripod masts. She was our home. We lived and ate and slept in her; we cared for her engines, decks, and guns. She had never fired a shot in anger, not even in World War I. Her cruising speed was only ten knots or so, but when she left the Golden Gate behind and began to push her ponderous bulk into the Pacific swells, you could feel her strength.

The *Oklahoma* seemed as reluctant to leave as the sailors who stood on her decks taking a long last look at the land they were leaving behind.

The last living land creatures we saw were the sea lions who lived on the rocks of the Farallon Islands, just off the California coast.

As the ship plowed on towards her rendezvous with history at Pearl Harbor, sailors quickly got used to being at sea again. It was almost a relief to get away from the various temptations that one found ashore, at least for a while until we could gather the strength to deal with the bright lights and pretty girls again. Which would be about a week, we figured, and most put San Francisco behind us to look forward to Honolulu. The wooden decks were washed and scrubbed, paint work cleaned, all the hundred and one details performed that would make the Okie the best-looking battleship in Battleships, Battle Force, we hoped. The rest of the battleships at Pearl would give us a critical eye when we entered port in a few days. Those men in the 4th deck division who weren't employed, were on watch—lifeboat, lookout, a wheel watch on the bridge, a few security watches.

The gunner's mates of turret 4 trained out their 14-inch guns, checking the turret thoroughly now that we were out of drydock and back in business once again. They'd done this a couple of times while at anchor in San Francisco; the gunner's mates had swung the great guns around to train them dead center on a couple of Japanese merchantmen in port, probably loaded with scrap iron. Just to shake them up a little. They were given the word not to do this anymore. Immediately the sailor's favorite epithet, useful in any situation, echoed down through the turret, "Fuck 'em!"

It was not clear who was meant—the Japanese, the ship's officers who had ordered them to stop, or no one in particular.

20

~~

Up on the surface, the sailors who had gotten off the ship were not out of danger yet. The attack was still going on in full fury. Dive-bombers and high-level bombers were following up the torpedo-plane attack on Battleship Row. American antiaircraft gunners were now in action, throwing black puffs of shrapnel high in the air. Some enemy planes were hit and plummeted down over the harbor, leaving fiery trails behind.

Ships exploded, burned, sank, trying to escape the boiling cauldron. The towering smoke of the funeral pyres rose high in the warm Hawaiian morning to blot out the sun. The air was torn asunder by the screaming planes with red circles on their wings and by the defender's guns that searched them out.

It was a mad, chaotic scene.

Swimming hard across the harbor toward the submarine base, Jack Miller tried to get away from the burning, sinking ships. He was still frustrated, angry that he could do nothing to fight off the attacking enemy planes. He kept looking back and watched the *Oklahoma* roll over and sink. No more *Oklahoma,* he thought. He could see Japanese planes making strafing runs down Battleship Row.

On the other side of Ford Island, the old battleship *Utah,* now a target ship, moored at one of the carrier berths, was torpedoed and bombed. Like the *Oklahoma,* she capsized and sank in less than fifteen minutes, taking fifty-eight sailors of her crew with her.

Miller watched the high-level bombers come over and drop one dead center on the *Arizona,* exploding a foward magazine. The Japanese had rigged a bomb out of an armor-piercing shell and it went right down through the forecastle near turret no. 2. Other bombs crashed into her superstructure. It looked to him as if one went right down her stack.

The *Arizona* was a total loss; 1,117 officers and men—four-fifths of her complement—lost their lives.

Then Miller got picked up by a boat that was heading for the sub base beach. A big black man hauled him out of the water; he must have been an officers' mess attendant. Whoever he was, the sailor had made a life-long friend of Miller. He'd about had it when the rescue boat picked him up.

He was a long way from Bremerton and that hotel. Wrapped in an Indian blanket, he had had to pick up a fire extinguisher and threaten to spray the lobby before the desk clerk would give him a nickel so he could call the ship and get his cousin, Merle Miller, to bring him another uniform.

When Miller hit the beach, someone gave him a Springfield rifle and he started popping away at the low-flying aircraft. He tried, but as far as he could tell, he didn't hit anything.

Ensign Rommel was picked up by a *West Virginia* motor launch, then eventually shifted over to a boat from the hospital ship *Solace* and took charge of the latter boat's rescue effort. During this time both Rommel and the boat crews did a good job picking up survivors in the water. It was heartbreaking work. Some of the sailors were okay, some were wounded and badly burned from the burning oil in the water, some were dead. Most of them were covered with oil, which made their bodies slippery and difficult to get into the boat.

Red Templeton was also fished out of the water by the *West Virginia's* motor launch and for a time assisted Rommel and the boat crew in helping others into the boat.

Dick Whitman was in the water near the motor launch. He saw Ensign Rommel directing rescue operations. Red Templeton was with him. He saw the launch stop to pick up a group of men in the water and watched them being pulled into the boat. Then it was his turn. Everyone else in the immediate area had been hauled out of the water.

But Whitman couldn't get up out of water and over the bow of the launch. The rescuers couldn't hold on to him, he was so oily. And he was getting tired.

Templeton said "Let's get the hell out of here!"

"Don't leave me," Whitman implored.

Rommel said, "There's Whitman, we've got to pick him up. Throw him a life jacket." He told Whitman to put a leg through the armhole and heave up. Dick tried to stick his foot and leg in. He was excited and exhausted.

"Stick your foot in, you dumb son of a bitch," Templeton yelled at Whitman.

They tried to pull him up but the arm strap broke and Whitman went back in the water.

Templeton threw the life jacket back at him and yelled, "The hell with him; let's go!"

Whitman stuck his foot and leg through the other armhole and they hauled him up and over the side onto the covered engine head and he tumbled down into the boat. He was thankful to be there.

The boat was full. He noticed John Sears, the boatswain's mate. Sears was throwing up. Marion Athas was in the boat.

Rommel said, "Let's take her across to Magazine Island." As they approached, he added, "Don't everybody run off. I want volunteers to go back and pick up some more men."

The rescued sailors dressed only in oil-soaked skivvies got out of the boat, glad to be ashore and safe for the moment.

Thanks to Mr. Rommel and no thanks to Red Templeton, Dick Whitman was still alive. Rommel returned to carry on his rescue efforts. Templeton had had enough.

Many other small boats from many different ships were now assisting in the rescue effort, including Coxswain Joe Hydrusko in a boat from the *Solace* and Ensign Joe Damrow, from the light cruiser *Honolulu,* who volunteered to officer that ship's no. 1 motor launch. The *Honolulu* had had her bow stove in when a bomb came crashing down through the pier to explode in the water alongside. The explosion had wreaked havoc in the forward 6-inch magazines and it was a miracle that the magazine didn't blow up, as the *Arizona*'s had.

Damrow ordered the coxswain to take the launch into the maelstrom along Battleship Row. "Over there, Patty," he directed the sailor, spotting the upturned hull of the *Oklahoma*. They were able to take off some men stranded on the Okie's bottom.

Down the line to the *West Virginia* and then the wreck of the *Arizona*. They pulled more sailors from the burning oil on the water . . . injured, burned, dead. They had almost forty in the launch now.

The launch had room for maybe ten more. Overhead the Japanese planes continued their strafing.

"We've got to get out of here," Damrow said to himself. "We can't stay here any longer; the launch is burning in several places. It's taking some water."

Tortured by the decision he had to make, Damrow ordered the boat to leave. Men were burning in oil. "No one can save them . . . awful . . . I feel guilty about leaving them; maybe we can save a few more. But the boat is burning; if we don't go, we'll lose everyone."

Patty, the cox'n, took the launch and its casualties to a safer place. He and the boat crew had performed an outstanding piece of rescue work.

For Joe Damrow, the judgment call was the hardest thing he ever did; the memory of it would haunt him always.

Rommel and Templeton were landed at Magazine Island. Templeton was running around without clothes on and Rommel was only partially clothed, having removed his blouse. Their whites were covered with oil. Then they were taken to the sub base.

One of the men picked out of the water was Marion Athas. His division officer, Rommel, was in the motor launch at the time and Athas watched him help sailors into the boat. Then it was his turn. I wouldn't have made it if it wasn't for Mr. Rommel, he thought, when he was safely in the launch.

Athas had let go his precarious hold on the floating seaplane, thinking it wouldn't hold up with so many people on it. He had left its limited security and struck out for shore. Looking back, he saw that the seaplane was going under, sinking. He heard calls for help, but there was nothing he could do. A man was lucky to keep himself afloat, he thought. Now that the initial shock of the attack was over, Athas realized what fear was. Then Rommel fished him out of the water—just in time.

Harold Johnson, who had been hanging on to the sinking plane's pontoon, was also picked up by one of the rescue launches. A Jap plane came over and strafed the launch, but the boat full of survivors finally landed at the sub base. Johnson headed for the showers to get the oil off.

Clayton McQuay could also feel the *Oklahoma*'s seaplane settling underneath them. Then he saw a whaleboat floating by, bottom up. McQuay swam to it, got up on it, and straddled it. It sank. He started to swim toward Merry Point. Could he make it? He couldn't swim that well.

Then a launch came by picking people out of the water. His good friend Oley Oleson was in it.

"Hey, Oleson, come alongside!" yelled McQuay. The launch did and the grinning Oleson, happy to see Mac was out okay, snaked him into the boat, hooking his fingers in McQuay's.

Just a moment before, Oleson had got Chief "Mollie" Newman out of the water, too. And for good measure, at least one sailor from the 3rd division, a gunner's mate third class, Billy Dale Boyd. Oleson pulled him out of the oily mess when he thought he was done for.

After telling the men in the turret to abandon ship, Oleson had had a busy time of it. First, he'd fished Athas out of the water after he'd got tangled up in the winch; then he'd managed to get over to the seaplane floating nearby. After being picked up by a passing boat, he had pulled Newman to safety, and then McQuay. And then Billy Dale Boyd—number five.

For a small man who could barely stretch his way into the navy—and couldn't swim—the first class turret captain had done pretty well for himself, and his shipmates. It will never be known exactly how many were able to escape from the turret because he went back in to tell them to abandon ship.

McQuay and the others were landed on the fueling docks on Ford Island. They were covered with oil. An officer said to get some clothes on and get cleaned up. This was the navy they were used to—everything clean and white. They went over to the barracks and got a change of clothing. Bombs were still falling and every time they'd hear one fall, they'd pile under the mess tables for protection.

Lying on the exposed bottom of the capsized *Oklahoma* was not a place to stay for long, and finally a motor launch took Shadow Bergstrom and some others, a number of them injured, over to Ford Island nearby. When they found a pickup truck with the key still in the ignition, they piled in, Jim Stallings at the wheel and Bergstrom in the cab with him. Stallings drove like mad to the dispensary where the medical people looked at the injured men, who were covered with oil and could hardly see.

At the dispensary, rescuers were bringing in the wounded and burned from the *Arizona* and other ships. It was a square building with a courtyard in the center. A Japanese plane dropped a bomb into the center of the yard, but no one was hit. The blast blew up and over them.

Stanton Jones, up from the handling room via the trunk, had jumped in the water when the ship was about ninety degrees over and was lying on her side. He got over to the floating seaplane, which sank almost at once.

Jones swam over to Ford Island. He was covered with oil. After prowling around a bit, he went over to the infirmary, which was immediately bombed. A piece of shrapnel cut into his hip. But the worst of the attack was over.

Small boats had been picking up men in the water around the seaplane, and the tall seaman from the state of Oklahoma, Everett Gunning, hung on, watching the strafing Jap planes while the seaplane sunk lower in the water. Finally, there were only three or four men left. No boats had come along for some time. Now, the pontoon was sinking. Gunning asked some of the men to help him get up on the pontoon and they did. Then Gunning hung his arms and legs over so that they could hold on to him and stay above water.

Finally, a small boat came along from the direction of fleet landing. A young sailor nearby swam to the boat. He had a crew cut and no clothes on, Gunning noticed. The boat crew couldn't get him out of the water because of all the oil on him. The sailor drowned right there in front of them.

Standing on the pontoon, Gunning waited for another boat to come by, then dived head first into the boat when it got close enough. No one else was in the water near them at the moment that he could see. Fire was on the water, surrounding them. The boat got out of there and headed for fleet landing. Every few moments, Gunning and the others just rescued would take off another piece of oil-soaked clothing, until, finally, they were all naked. As soon as they got ashore, they headed for the showers to clean up.

They were in the showers when all at once a boatswain's mate still in his liberty dress whites stuck his head in the showers and yelled, "Get the hell out of the shower! Don't you know there a fucking war on?" His face was flushed. Whether from excitement or strong drink, they weren't quite sure.

The survivors of the sunken ships just looked at him.

21

$\mathbf{A}$l Sandall was one of those who made it to the floating plane and he hung on to its propeller for dear life. Despite his predicament, he was able to find something amusing in watching some of the Okie's crew walk or scramble around the hull as she capsized.

But the plane was knocked under water and was filling rapidly. Finally, only the pontoon was still on top—the same one that was supporting Gunning. Sandall let go of the propeller and came alongside the pontoon. Men were clinging to it. It seemed to Al that there was a foot of crude oil on the water. Sailors were hanging on anything that would float. Rescue boats tried to throw life jackets to the sailors struggling for their lives in that sea of oil and water.

Japanese planes were still coming in over the top of them, the rear gunners spraying everything in sight. Things looked bad from where Sandall kept his precarious hold on the seaplane.

Then the high-level bombers came over and Sandall watched the *Arizona* go up. Among the sailors who died in that proud ship was Mike Sandall, his cousin.

Sandall and the sailors in the water near him were downwind from the burning *Arizona,* and the fire was spreading over the water in their direction. They yelled for the boats to pick them up.

Sandall was picked out of the water by a twenty-six footer and taken to fleet landing along with Gunning. People there, mostly navy yard workers, still didn't realize this was war, not some sort of exercise.

It dawned on Gunning all at once that he had no clothes on. He asked Sandall, "What do I do now, Al?" looking at all the people on fleet landing.

Sandall replied, "Don't worry. No one knows you from Adam." Gunning, reassured, walked up through the crowd, a bit uncomfortable nevertheless.

They got to the receiving barracks, where they showered, first using gasoline to get the oil off their faces and out of their hair. They were a mess, but they were alive.

The survivors were given clothes to wear, and then they went into the mess hall, where they were still serving chow, even with the attack going on. Their uniforms were a mixture of anything they could get hold of. Then they were ordered over to dry dock no. 1 to fight the fires raging on the *Pennsylvania, Cassin,* and *Downes.* The men spread out to make it more difficult for strafing planes.

Dick Whitman was in this group. He had acquired a skivvy shirt, white trousers, and sneakers and felt better dressed. The second wave of Japanese planes came over. They could see the tracer bullets and dived for cover. Someone had a radio on. The radio was saying the Japanese were attacking. It seemed rather strange to hear this, thought the Okie's gunner's mate.

Bob Lewis, out of the chiefs' quarters with his three companions, helped to pick up sailors out of the water for a time. There were several life rafts floating loose, which were gathered in and tied behind the motor launch. Men coming up out of the water climbed on, and the boat headed for the sub base, towing the life rafts astern. Blood trickled through the oil that covered Lewis. The others insisted he needed first aid. But his wounds were not serious, just cuts and scratches.

Stretched out on the bottom of the capsized Okie, Norman Wiley was in bad shape with his broken arm and leg. Finally, he was picked up by a motor whaleboat. The crew rightly figured he needed help. Wiley was unable to talk to them clearly. They rolled him on his stomach, stuck his broken arm under his head and commenced to give him artificial respiration.

Wiley kept trying to drag his broken arm from under his head but they wouldn't let him. It hurt like hell. So did his leg. His face burned and so did his hands and shoulders. The guys in the boat almost killed Wiley while trying to save him, but meant well.

Finally, they got him to Ford Island and into the sickbay there. Then the second wave of Japanese planes came over and the pharmacist's mates and hospital corpsmen jerked the injured men off their beds, put them underneath, and covered them with mattresses.

How many shots of morphine had they given him? The corpsmen had put a big M on his forehead, but, the way he was sweating and rubbing his forehead, how could they know? Wiley was pretty well out of it anyway, morphine or no morphine. He hurt all over and he was scared. Planes were strafing now. The sickbay sounded like a hornet's nest. Every so often, Wiley could feel something hit the mattress. Finally, the morphine got to him and he didn't even know it when the corpsmen put him back in his bed.

Swimming out into the harbor away from Battleship Row, Arthur Claudmantle saw a fifty-foot motor launch picking up sailors out of the water. The boat crew didn't see him, though, and the Connecticut petty officer swam toward it. Every time he'd get close, the cox'n would ring the bell and the boat would move off, then stop again. And then the process would be repeated. Claudmantle chased the boat almost across the harbor as it headed for the mine dock. His other choice would have been to swim for Ford Island, but there was too much oil on the water.

He just couldn't catch up with the boat. It seemed as if he had swum five miles. Then when the boat was only fifty yards from the mine dock, the crew saw him. They got hold of Claudmantle by the hair and flipped him over the side like a big fish. The boat had no seats in it. As soon as they got him over the side, the sailors turned him loose and he tumbled down to the bottom of the boat. It hurt worse than anything else that had happened to him for the past half hour or so since the attack began.

Painfully, Claudmantle raised up and looked out across the harbor. He saw something in the water close at hand. It looked like a coconut. Only there were two lidded white eyes looking at him. The coconut went under, then surfaced. Three times. The heavily lidded white eyes just looked at them, then blinked slowly, once or twice.

"It's a guy!" shouted Claudmantle. The sailors got him up into the boat. It was a man named Jackson, an *Oklahoma* boatswain's mate.

"Jesus, I'll never drink another Goddamn beer again in my life," said the exhausted sailor.

All of a sudden, everyone started laughing hysterically. They couldn't seem to stop. The shock of the attack had gone in the humor of the moment.

The survivors were let out at the mine dock and were on their own. All Claudmantle had on was the ring around the neck of his skivvy shirt, his bos'n's pipe around his neck, and his skivvy shorts.

There were a couple of minor confrontations with some nervous marines. Then Claudmantle and his companions saw an Oriental man with an automobile. The sailors told the frightened man that they were commandeering his car to go to the receiving ship, where they would report for duty. The man wouldn't let them climb on the running boards of his shiny new car unless they used rags to hold on so they wouldn't get the car dirty.

They couldn't believe it. There was a war on and this guy was worried about getting his car dirty! It was true that they were covered with oil, but you'd think a dirty car wouldn't matter under the circumstances. There were some strong words. Then, all at once, the man took off at fifty miles per hour. All the way to the receiving ship, Claudmantle and friends were hanging on for dear life, trying not to get their oily hand prints all over the shiny car.

At the receiving station, they finally got into the showers, washed off the oil with cans of paint thinner, and then broke into the navy exchange to get some clothes. Art got a pair of brown and white shoes and grabbed some pants from a nearby clothesline.

Then the Okie survivors, like Sandall and his group, were sent off to fight the fires on the ships in no. 1 dry dock.

Captain Foy, the former skipper of the *Oklahoma,* whom they all liked and who had been transferred ashore a few months ago to await further assignment, was there. He told them, "Stick together, men. I'll get another ship and put the *Oklahoma*'s crew on it."

No one knew where Captain Bode, the present skipper, was.

22

O ut in the harbor on the sea sled, as soon as he got over feeling sorry for his broken finger, Rufus Nance started thinking of how he could get out of there and save his life, never mind his finger. A few moments later, a rescue motor launch came by and began taking men aboard, Nance among them. The oil-covered sailors were using life jackets and anything else that was available to keep themselves afloat.

Nance saw a Japanese plane come over them. The plane released three bombs, which appeared to be headed straight for the launch. A few men swore in frustration; most didn't say anything because they were in a state of shock, their minds numbed.

Oily faces turned skyward; the survivors saw the bombs hit the water some distance away.

The rescue launch, loaded with sailors, headed across the harbor toward the submarine base. When they arrived, everyone except the crew got out of the launch and headed for the barracks. Nance, Spaulding, Glen Raymond, and Sandall, all together, washed the oil off their bodies as best they could with soap and water in the barracks washroom. The almost naked men were then told to go to the "lucky bag" for some clothing.

Nance was large, broad across the middle, and hard to fit. He got into a dungaree shirt with sleeves that only reached halfway down his arms and had to be tied with a string to close the front. The dungaree pants fit him the same way, with trouser bottoms halfway up his legs. They, too, had to be secured with string in the front. Nance felt ridiculous, but considering the circumstances, things could be worse.

Back in the harbor, near Battleship Row, sailors in the water looked up at the high-altitude bombers coming in over them. Westley Potts counted five. The men cheered as the antiaircraft gunners on the ships tried desperately to reach the enemy planes. Black puffs of exploding AA shells covered the sky. The planes were too high for the guns and moved off untouched. They had released their bombs and Potts watched them hit just astern of the upturned bottom of the *Oklahoma*. One hit forward of the *West Virigina* and another hit her but did not explode. Then he saw two more hit the *Arizona*. Fire and smoke from the ship towered high in the air.

Potts saw twenty-five or thirty men up in the foremast of the *Arizona*. Fire was all around them now. He could see they were trying to come down the mast, but they were blocked by the roaring flames. Shocked and horrified by the sight of the doomed *Arizona* sailors, Potts watched while some of them jumped into the fiery water far below them, while others stayed where they were. High in the mast, they were roasted alive as the flames reached up and consumed them.

Several men in the water nearby were hit by shrapnel. Potts was nicked, but it was not serious. He looked at the jagged scratch that the piece of metal had left on his left arm. He noticed that a gunner's mate near him was getting tired, and he gave the man some of his wood flotsam to stay afloat. Someone yelled, "We better get out of here! This oil is going to burn!" It seemed logical to Potts as he looked at the fire on the water spreading out toward them from the burning *Arizona*.

He started swimming around the protruding stern of the capsized *Oklahoma* and then an *Argonne* motor launch stopped to pick him up out of the water. Finally! But the crew couldn't pull the slippery Potts up over the bow and he wasn't much help, either, at this point. "Get me up over the stern; it's lower in the water," Potts told his rescuers. They did, and he was on board and safe for the moment.

Potts helped to pull some of the other men out of the water. The launch went alongside the upturned *Oklahoma*; there were several sailors in the water close to her. One of them was William Pask, a fireman from the Okie, who had been operated on for the removal of his appendix in sickbay just yesterday. Pharmacist's mates William E. Duncan (2d class) and Kenneth M. Dean (3d class) had loaded him on a stretcher and managed to get him up high enough in the ship so with the aid of still other men, he could jump and save himself as the *Oklahoma* rolled over. Pask passed out as soon as they got him into the launch. It was understandable.

The launch also picked up an Okie sailor named Showalter. He was joking and laughing, relieved to be rescued. "I was about to let loose," he told his rescuers. "I was too tired to hold on much longer."

The sailor who was acting as cox'n of the *Argonne*'s launch had never run one before, and he asked if there was anyone in the boat with any experience. Potts spoke up and said he had, so the inexperienced coxswain, who had been doing pretty well, turned the boat over to the more experienced second class boatswain's mate from the Okie.

Potts took the launch around by the bow of the damaged *West Vir-*

ginia, searching for men to pick up. The *West Virginia* was down by the bow, settling toward the harbor bottom. Her great anchor was secured at the hawsepipe in her side. A sailor was sitting on the anchor, his feet dangling in the water. He looked lonely there but seemed safe for the moment, and Potts started to take the launch down between the *West Virginia* and the battleship *Tennessee*, alongside, where the oil on the water was on fire, to see if they could save anyone. He would then go back and get the fellow from his perch on the anchor. After looking around for a minute or two, Potts took the launch back to the sinking bow of the *West Virginia,* but the sailor was gone. He was relieved to hear some time later that another boat had taken the man off and that he was okay.

The crew of the "Weevie" as her sailors nicknamed her, was abandoning ship. Potts brought his launch alongside to help. Several sailors were lying dead on deck; others were just knocked out. He also noticed a few of the ships's officers walking around in a daze. Like zombies, Potts thought. He could tell that they were in shock because the officers were still trying to get the life rafts off the ship although there were several motor launches standing by to take the men off. Potts's crew picked up one of the unconscious sailors, and then Potts decided to return to the *Argonne* to unload.

Back at the *Argonne,* Potts tried to carry the injured sailor up the gangway but couldn't manage it. The man's body was just too oily. Several men pitched in and got the sailor aboard while Potts, the engineer, and the seaman bow hook stayed in the launch.

Now the Japanese came over the harbor again with another wave of planes. There were dive-bombers everywhere, it seemed to Potts. The planes looked like they were coming straight down at them. All of the ships, recovering now from their initial surprise, were pouring up a storm of antiaircraft fire. Potts couldn't believe that the planes were able to get through. And some of them didn't, crashing into the water or nearby shore. Potts and his crew watched a destroyer tied up near the *Argonne* depress her 5-inch antiaircraft gun too low and when she fired, the shell blew off the Union Jack on the "tin can" next to her.

For awhile, the crew lay flat on the bottom of the launch, waiting for the storm to pass over. Would they survive, or would their launch go up in splinters, and they along with it? It was apparent to the boat crew that the planes were still going after the big ships and even though the *Argonne* as an auxiliary was smaller than the battleships and cruisers, she still qualified in size.

The Japanese planes kept coming so Potts decided to get away from the *Argonne.* He shoved off and took the launch out in the harbor where there weren't any ships close by. It was about 0900.

From their viewing area in the channel, Potts and his boat crew watched in awe as the mighty *Nevada* made her famous sortie out of the harbor, the only battleship to get under way that morning and despite the torpedo that had torn a hole in her side, well forward.

The *Nevada* was putting up a tremendous fight of it as she drew opposite 1010 dock where the *Oglala* had been sunk and the *Helena* damaged. Despite the carnage of battle all around them, the sailors in the launch thrilled at the sight of the huge battlewagon as she attempted to get out the channel, her bow pointing to the open sea beyond.

Colored flags whipped at her signal hoists; the stars and stripes of her battle flag flew high above her decks. Every enemy plane that could, went after the *Nevada* in an all-out effort to stop her, to sink her in the channel and bottle up the harbor. Every gun except her 14-inch was firing and it appeared to Potts that she got several of the attacking aircraft.

Bombs crashed down—at least five—to smash into the battleship's decks and superstructure. One gun crew and part of another were wiped out. Spray from near misses towered in the air to merge with her smoke, and from time to time the *Nevada* was almost obscured from those who watched.

The *Nevada* didn't make it out to sea and probably it was just as well. Hit again and again and badly damaged, her decks afire, the gallant ship was ordered to beach herself so there would be no chance of her sinking in the channel. She came to rest in the mud off Hospital Point, her guns still firing. Tugs were ordered to help put out her fires with water hoses and to assist her in her movement across the channel to a more permanent beaching off Waipio Point.

The *Nevada* was out of it now, but she would live to fight again and so would most of her crew. As brave as the ship and men who manned her were, however, the actions of the senior officer on board, Lieutenant Commander Francis J. Thomas, U.S. Naval Reserve, who took her out, were particularly worthy of attention. Her chief quartermaster, who steered her down the channel, also deserved note.

Westley Potts thought he would never see anything quite so spectacular again.

While the *Nevada* was on her way, Japanese aircraft went after the battleship *Pennsylvania* in dry dock no. 1. Potts watched a bomb crash into the ship and blow off one of the broadside guns, he thought. More bombs came crashing into the destroyers *Cassin* and *Downes,* just forward of the *Pennsylvania* in the dry dock. The two destroyers were ripped apart, on fire despite the flooding of the dry dock, and the *Cassin* was leaning over against the *Downes.*

It seemed everything was happening at once. The destroyer *Shaw* was hit in the floating dry dock about the same time, around 0915.

Then, about 0930, Potts and the crew saw a tremendous fiery explo-

The *Oklahoma* (BB-37) passing under Golden Gate Bridge in San Francisco, about 1927. Note 5-inch/51-caliber AA guns on the bridge alongside no. 2 turret (trained forward). (Courtesy USS *Oklahoma* Association)

Company 10, Naval Training Station Newport, R.I., August 1940. Among those who were assigned to the battleship *Oklahoma* were Slapikas, Raskulimecz, Young, Vidito, and Savage. CQM Meadows, company commander, *in front.* Numbering rows 1–7 from the front: *row 4, first on left,* Edward F. Slapikas;

row 3, third from left, George Raskulimecz; *row 7, fifth from left*, Stephen B. Young; *row 1, third from left*, Chief Meadows; *row 4, third from right*, Lyal J. Savage; *row 6, eighth from left*, Raymond Vidito; *row 6, ninth from left*, Herbert W. Jones, Jr.; *row 6, second from right*, Warren Allen. (S. B. Young)

Company 11, Naval Training Station, Newport, R.I., August 1940. Among those who went to the *Oklahoma* were Turcotte, Scolamiero, and Savarese. Numbering rows 1–7 from the front: *row 5, first from left,* Louis Scolamiero; *row 2, first from left,* Rudolph A. Turcotte; *row 3, fifth from left,* Michael J. Savarese. (Courtesy Louis Scolamiero)

Norman E. Wiley, Sea 1/c

Clarence J. Mullaley, Sea 1/c

Arthur Claudmantle, Jr., BM 2/c

Mary Claudmantle (Courtesy Arthur Claudmantle, Jr.)

William P. Schauf, Sea 2/c

Russell M. Davenport, Sea 1/c

Left, Stephen B. Young, Sea 1/c, and Michael J. Savarese, Sea 1/c (S. B. Young)

Stephen B. Young, Sea 1/c

Michael J. Savarese, Sea 1/c
(Courtesy Michael J. Savarese)

Left, Wilbur T. Hinsperger, and friend (Courtesy Mrs. Wilbur T. Hinsperger)

Frank H. Scott, Sea 1/c

Stanton E. Jones, Sea 1/c

Everett G. Gunning, Sea 2/c

Wilbur T. Hinsperger (Courtesy
Mrs. Wilbur T. Hinsperger)

Harold E. Johnson, Sea 2/c

James E. Stallings, Sea 2/c

Albert F. Sandall, Cox

Rufus F. Nance, BM 2/c

Seaman Dick Whitman standing in front of the Army and Navy YMCA, Honolulu, 1938

Royal E. Bergstrom and his Australian girlfriend

Marion H. Athas, Sea 1/c

Coxswain Howard E. Roberts, Jr., as a Chief Petty Officer in 1944

The *Oklahoma*'s boxing team. *Second from left,* Westley F. Potts, Cox; *left,* Otis Johnson, MAT 3/c . (Courtesy Westley F. Potts)/

Left, Layton T. Banks, Cox. Died 7 December 1941 in the *Oklahoma*'s lamp locker. (Courtesy Albert F. Sandall)

Below, The *Oklahoma* and other battleships on fleet maneuvers in the Pacific, Spring 1938. (Courtesy USS *Oklahoma* Association)

Thanksgiving menu, USS *Oklahoma* 1941 (S. B. Young)

Hawaii

Thanksgiving
Luau
1941

★

U. S. S.
Oklahoma

★

Jack V. Miller, Sea 1/c, on his back, and Seaman Rudolph A. Turcotte, kneeling, Waikiki Beach, with the Royal Hawaiian Hotel in the background, 27 June 1941. (Courtesy Louis Scolamiero)

Fireman Ed Miller teases his cousin, Seaman Jack Miller, on the beach at Waikiki. Royal Hawaiian Hotel and other U.S. sailors in background. (Courtesy Louis Scolamiero)

Left, Fireman Ed Miller, Seaman Louis Scolamiero, and Seaman Rudolph A. Turcotte pose before the car in which they toured Oahu. (Courtesy Louis Scolamiero)

Below left: *from left,* Turk Turcotte, Jack Miller, Ed Miller, and Louis Scolamiero on the beach at Waikiki. Diamond Head in background. (Courtesy Louis Scolamiero)

Below right, Turcotte *(left)* and cousins Ed and Jack Miller (unknown friend at *right*). On a dry run with their outrigger at Waikiki. (Courtesy Louis Scolamiero)

Souvenir of a wild boar hunt. Turret Captain Roy Stewart holds the boar's head. Ensign Norman Hoffman, USNR, turret no. 2 officer, is at *left*. (Courtesy Norman Hoffman)

Some of the crew of turret no. 4 pose for the camera while the *Oklahoma* is at sea, about 1937. *Top row, left to right:* Harald R. A. Oleson, GM 2/c; Bernard G. Ragsdale, Sea 1/c; and Ernest L. Dexter, Cox. *Middle row, left to right:* Frederick D. or Forest A. Miller, Sea 1/c; Louis C. Templeton, Cox; and Joseph S. Oberman, Sea 1/c. *Bottom row, left to right:* Clayton W. McQuay, Sea 1/c; Roy Stewart, GM 2/c; and Ernest C. Ericson, GM 2/c.

Note the right arm rates and watchmarks on the shoulders of the seamen, especially the pointer's specialty insignia on the left arm of Miller, as well as the tiny *E* sewn on the right arms of Miller and Ragsdale. (Louis C. Templeton, courtesy USS *Oklahoma* Association)

The *Oklahoma* at Puget Sound Navy Yard, 28 September 1940. Note the "birdbath" atop the mainmast, a platform added for antiaircraft machine guns. Turrets no. 1 and 2 are prominent forward of the foremast, and turret no. 4 is visible aft. (Courtesy USS *Oklahoma* Association)

Left, Japanese photograph 7 December 1941 shows torpedo splash in water, *left.* Shock waves from previous hits show from the *Oklahoma, forward,* and the *West Virginia, next astern. From left to right* (sterns to left), ships are battleship (BB) *Nevada, Vestal* and BB *Arizona (forward,* starboard), BB *West Virginia* and BB *Tennessee (forward,* starboard), BB *Oklahoma* and BB *Maryland (forward,* starboard), and *Neosho. At the far right (center)* is BB *California.*

Looking out the harbor, Ford Island is to the *right* and the navy yard across the water to the *left.* The ships' bows point to the harbor entrance and the sea beyond. (Courtesy USS *Oklahoma* Association)

Below, The *Oklahoma* capsized, the *Maryland* inboard. Smoke and fires rage along Battleship Row, 7 December 1941. (Courtesy USS *Oklahoma* Association)

The *Oklahoma*'s captain's gig alongside the upturned hull as the rescue effort begins, 7 December 1941. The *Maryland* is alongside. (Courtesy USS *Oklahoma* Association)

The capsized *Oklahoma* from astern, with rescue party organizing to free men trapped below. Note propeller protruding from the water and the *Maryland* alongside, 7 December 1941. (Courtesy USS *Oklahoma* Association)

Mrs. Elmer E. Young
73 No. Lowell St.
Methuen
Massachusetts

U.S.A.

USS *Oklahoma* postmarks,
1940–41

Hospital ship USS *Solace* postmark, 1941

Below, The *Oklahoma* being rolled upright by means of winches from Ford Island (*out of view, to left*). Looking aft, sailor balances on turret no. 1. Aiea and Pearl City are across the harbor, in background. (National Archives)

Inset, Unloading 5-inch shells from magazine after the *Oklahoma* had been righted and pumped out. (National Archives)

Richard F. Whitman, GM 2/c, first of WWII servicemen to join Hibbing, Minn., V.F.W. Post, February 1942.

Water-soaked dollar bill bet with Wilbur Hinsperger while trapped below after the *Oklahoma* capsized. The author has carried it ever since as a souvenir of the experience.

sion as the *Shaw* blew up when hit once more. Fireworks to end all fireworks, Potts thought, as the sailors in the boat watched in stunned amazement. The dry dock sank and so did what remained of the *Shaw*.

Then a bomb hit near the *California*'s bow, throwing a huge geyser of water in the air. The *California* was the foremost ship in Battleship Row, where the *Nevada* had been the last. One of the Japanese planes, leaving a long trail of smoke behind, came down to crash into the side of the seaplane tender *Curtiss*. Earlier, the tender had shot off the conning tower—and supposedly the captain's head—of a Japanese midget submarine in the harbor. The sub got off a torpedo at the tender, but that was the last thing it did except blow up and sink when the destroyer *Monaghan* ran it down and depth charged it.

Potts watched a plane blow up over Ford Island and disintegrate.

After the second attack was over, Potts and his intrepid crew went around the channel with their launch picking up survivors from the sinking ships. They fished out one sailor who had fallen off a tugboat while trying to free a line that had somehow got entangled in the tug's screw.

Potts took the boat alongside the burning *Arizona* to see if there were any possible survivors. All they found was a pair of officer's pants, hastily discarded by whoever had been wearing them. There was seventy-five cents in the pockets.

There were no more men to be taken from the water near the ship, so Potts looked around for something else. He noticed a life raft in the water, just forward of the fire that was sweeping down Battleship Row. Potts decided to get it out of the way and went alongside the raft to take it in tow.

A black man was sitting in oil in the life raft, almost up to his neck, it seemed to Potts. All the crew could see were the whites of his eyes. They told him, "Come on, get in." The frightened sailor said, "No, I want to stay here." Potts and the crew had to rescue him forcibly; the fire was drawing too close for comfort.

Fire was sweeping down on the damaged and sinking *California* and it was decided to abandon ship. It seemed to Potts that there were at least a couple of hundred sailors in the water, swimming for shore. Potts, thinking that the fire in the water put these men in great danger, ran his motor launch around in circles, kicking up a backwash that cleared a space in the burning oil and keeping the fire from consuming the frightened men.

Cox'n Potts kept this up for almost too long. The fire was making such a noise that the boat engineer couldn't hear the bells by which Potts signaled the speeds he wanted. The boat had just finished making a circle and was coming around for another one, when Potts saw he couldn't make it. He gave the bells to back down, but the engineer didn't hear them. The man they had just pulled off the raft was lying down, up in the bow of the launch. When he saw that the boat was about to go into the fire, he rose to his knees, raised his hands in the air and said, "Oh, Lord. Don't go in there!" Potts was plenty scared himself.

But the engineer could see, even if he didn't hear the bells. He backed down, finally. When the launch slowed, and they were away from the immediate danger, the engineer said, "I backed her down like she ain't never been backed down before." The others in the crew agreed. The black man in the bow sank down in the boat again.

Now Potts brought the launch alongside the *California* and the indomitable crew of the *Argonne's* motor launch, cox'n'd by an *Oklahoma* sailor, took two loads of men ashore. Many had their clothes burned off, and it looked as though some had their eyes burned out. On the water, the fire had turned and gone down the port side of the ship. Potts and the crew felt sure that they had checked it from engulfing the sailors in the water a few moments before. Potts figured they had saved quite a few men from getting their pants scorched.

Potts and his crew finally brought the launch back to the *Argonne* and got the oil off their bodies as best they could, using diesel oil from the launch and rags and some sand they had in the launch to keep from slipping around. It was rough on the skin, so they went aboard to shower. The *Argonne's* crew opened their lockers and gave Potts and the others whatever clothes they needed. Potts also appropriated a pair of shoes he saw on the deck outside the sickbay, where he had gone to have his eyes treated. He figured the man who owned them wouldn't be needing them for awhile.

He left the *Argonne* and went over to the receiving station. Several men were wandering around naked and drinking coffee while receiving medical attention. Although there were a few women around, they didn't seem to notice anything unusual about this. Potts was issued another pair of shoes and dungarees and was given something to eat. By now, the *Oklahoma* boatswain's mate was feeling pretty bad and had a headache. After having done all he could for the time being, he drew some bedding and went to sleep. Westley Potts had put in a good morning's work.

PART 4

Keep Silence about the Decks

23

$\sim$

The chaos of burning ships in the harbor above was unknown to those of us who were trapped below in the *Oklahoma*. We had just begun our long ordeal.

When Bob Roberts returned to the trunk space from his unsuccessful exploration of the nearby compartments, he heard some interesting news. Someone said that a man had disappeared underwater from the trunk and hadn't come back.

Where did he go? It was something to think about. Did he find a way out? Or was he blocked somehow in his attempt to escape—hung up— caught on something? It might be worth a try. Roberts didn't know whether to "blow tubes or draw small stores," as the saying goes on the mess decks.*

Clarence Mullaley had been aware in the darkness there that someone had tried to go down the water-filled escape hatch in the trunk. Two, he thought, when the light was flashed briefly around the trunk—a couple of blond-haired guys. It was difficult to say, it was so dark down here, and the occasional use of the battle lantern made it seem that much worse when the light went out. Was one of the them the sailor who had grabbed him up out of harm's way back there in the handling room? Savarese, maybe? But he was dark-haired. In any event, they hadn't come back. Someone said to turn out the light so that the batteries would last longer.

It was quiet there in the trunk. San Antonio was a long way away thought Mullaley. He'd almost joined the CCC,† but he'd heard Walter Winchell say over the radio that if a young man joined the navy when he was seventeen, he could complete a minority enlistment when he was only twenty-one. So, he'd gone and signed up. In boot camp the cooks had told him to drink all the milk he could from the big vats in the mess hall; he might not get another chance.

Chances didn't look too good right now.

Time drifted by. We sat on the inclined ladder or stretched out as best we could to keep out of the water below us. There was little talk. The

---

*A high degree of confusion. Sailors purchased shoes and articles of clothing from the ship's small stores. Blowing tubes was a function of the engineers, who blew the soot out of the boiler tubes on the average of once a day at sea. In wartime, this was done at night so enemy eyes could not see black smoke coming out of the stack.

†Civilian Conservation Corps.

water lapped gently against the top coaming of the watertight door leading into the trunk from the handling room.

I spoke up, asking of no one in particular, "What happened to Mr. Rommel? He said he was going to come back for us to let us know what was going on."

"Who knows?" said someone from out of the darkness. "Maybe he couldn't."

Another voice said, "He wouldn't just leave us here like this. Maybe the Japs got him."

"Yeah, he must be dead; he would have told us to abandon ship or something."

"Jesus, why did Rommel send us down below, anyway? We were safer up in the turret. Maybe we could have got out."

"Shit."

"What about the poor guys on the shell deck? And how they screamed? We'll never get out of this Goddamn place," someone said in resignation. "To hell with Rommel."

"Knock it off," someone said. It sounded like Red Aldridge. Didn't he have any ideas except to turn off the light or stop talking? He was the senior petty officer present, after all.

But no one as yet would speak of what we all felt, that we might very well die here, deep inside the ship. No one spoke about this because it would do no good.

It was eerie there, hearing the voices of unseen faces speaking out of the darkness of that watery tomb. Yet there was no panic. Only the oppressing resignation to what seemed like almost certain death.

Through it all, despite the apparent hopelessness of our situation, there ran a ray of hope, nothing that anyone could acknowledge as yet. Still, it was there—an undefinable something that told us to hang on—all was not lost.

We were still alive. That subconscious spark that wills a person to live, to never give up though all seems hopeless, was there in that place in varying degrees, depending on the man. Some thought of escape, some of rescue, others were resigned to whatever might be in store for them—even death. Most prayed silently for God to help in whatever way He could. We thought of home, our mothers and fathers, girl friends, or nothing at all.

I could almost feel the dark. The stillness of that deep and stinking place pressed down over us all. I felt I was smothering in the darkness there. Once in a while, a man would cough or move a little, and, every so often, I became aware of the barely perceptible sound of the water as it rose, ever so slowly.

Sometime later, out of the darkness—"Red Templeton pulled a gun on us up in the turret—a .45—and told us to get the hell back down like we were ordered," Wimpy Hinsperger, who was next to me, said bitterly. Several others heard and said this was true.

"Jesus Christ, he did? He pulled a gun?" I asked incredulously. "Where did he get it?"

"Who the hell knows?"

"I think I know," Wimpy said. "I figure Rommel gave it to him; he told Red to make sure we went below like he ordered."

"Jesus, why would he want to do that?"

"I don't know. Maybe he saw it in a movie," someone said.

"We would have made it out."

Yes, I thought, but it was too late now. Why? Rommel probably thought he was doing the right thing and it got to be too much for him.

"Frig Templeton too, the bastard," a voice said tiredly. No one said anything more.

Time drifted by. Almost all of us there realized the water was rising slowly, replacing the air that was gradually leaking out of the air pocket that surrounded us like a cocoon, keeping us alive. But no one spoke of this just yet.

"How about that broad-assed Spitler?" a voice asked. "He was running through the handling room like a bat out of hell."

"Scared shitless—like all of us."

"Yeah, but we manned our battle stations and he just took off."

"You should have seen him," the voice almost laughed. "He went up through the turret like he had a rough corn cob stuck up his ass."

I grinned at this old southern expression. It was favorite of the quick-tempered Chief Quartermaster Meadows, my company commander back at boot camp in Newport. With this and other colorful threats, Meadows encouraged the recruits in his company to try a little harder so that some day we might be sailors.

"To hell with them all. It doesn't matter now. We're stuck down here." Whoever it was, he spoke for us all.

"Quiet down, you guys; you're using up the air. No talking." Aldridge again.

I lay back on my steel perch and thought about the *Oklahoma*.

The easy-going Arthur Claudmantle, the boatswain's mate in charge of the division's topside crew, was one of the ones who indoctrinated me into the world of wire brushing, red leading, and painting various topside areas. These and other matters of elementary seamanship. I thought he had a lot of patience to deal with the newer seamen like me as we learned the ways of the navy.

One of Claudmantle's stories about his expeditions ashore still made me laugh. It was just before I'd come aboard.

The *Oklahoma* and other battleship sailors hung out at one particular tavern in Long Beach named George's. It was a large and noisy place, poorly lit but friendly, with plenty of booths, tables and chairs, a large bar, and a dance floor. It was a favorite spot to meet after going ashore— to have a few beers, talk shop, and tell sea stories. It was good to get off the ship.

Many sailors stayed put and eventually young ladies drifted in out of the night to sit at the booths and tables and dance with them. As the sailors of the Pacific Fleet put more beer down the hatch in the spirit of good fellowship, the talk grew louder. As the evening wore on, the establishment grew rougher and tougher. The shore patrol looked in at George's frequently.

This particular day in 1940, a number of Okie sailors, all in their dress blues, sat in George's, peacefully drinking beer. It was early yet. Arthur Claudmantle was there with some of the other petty officers from the ship—Al Holtel was one. There were seamen, firemen, and an assortment of sailors from other ships in the harbor.

Sitting at the bar by himself was a bos'n's mate from the *Oklahoma* named Bull Smith.* He looked the part. He had a dark beard and bashed in nose; his arms, and meaty hands, hung down to his knees almost. No one in the ship and very few ashore gave Bull Smith problems. Certainly not the seamen in his deck division. Bull was married and on his way home but decided to stop in for a couple of drinks. He had stayed too long and now he was drunk.

Suddenly, a large, angry-looking woman came bursting in through the door from the street outside. It was Bull Smith's wife.

She headed directly for the bar, breathing fire. All eyes turned toward her. But Smith did not see her.

Conversation stopped as the angry woman stormed across the gap between her and her wayward husband. This was domestic drama; all eyes in the bar were riveted on the scene.

Bull still hadn't spotted his wife—had just ordered another shot and beer. "Watch out!" said the bartender.

And then she was upon him. "You good for nothin' bum!" yelled Mrs. Smith. "In here drinkin' when you should be home with your wife and kids!"

Bull Smith turned on his bar stool to stare with glassy eyes. His wife! His shot glass was halfway up from the bar. His jaw dropped in complete surprise.

The bartender grinned. The appreciative audience of sailors smirked.

---

*Bull Smith was transferred to the *Utah* and was a survivor of the ship 7 December 1941.

Bull's wife looked around. "Wipe that stupid grin off your face, you jerk!" The bartender, no fool, did so. To the sailors, "What the hell are you lookin' at, you clowns?" They kept quiet. Mrs. Smith was as tough as Bull.

She turned again to her husband, who was still sitting there, mouth agape, his mind befogged. He drank some beer and belched.

"Oh, c'mon, honey. I jus' stopped in t' have a few," Bull slurred his words. "Nothin' wrong with that . . . had a tough day on the ship. God-damn officers, stupid swabbies."

"C'mon honey, have a drink." Bull patted the stool beside him. Amazingly, she hiked herself onto the barstool.

"A drink for my wife, bartender," ordered Smith. "Make it a double. On the double." He laughed uproariously.

She was still pissed off, but he would quiet her down. He lit up a cigarette with some difficulty and hung it in his mouth.

"Gimmee a big kiss, honey," Bull leered. He stuck his face over to give his wife a kiss. As he pressed his face to Mrs. Smith's, the lighted cigarette mashed into her mouth.

The sailors gasped. The bartender stopped breathing. Bull, horrified at what he had done, froze. A deadly quiet settled over the place.

Mrs. Smith turned red, then white, then purple as the pain increased. She yelled and swore through her burned lips, swung at Bull with all her strength, which just turned her around on her bar stool. Smith ducked. What had he done? Just when things were looking up.

Now she was off the stool. Spotting a gumball machine secured to a nearby bulkhead, she wrenched it off, her fury giving her the strength to do what none there could have done. Right out of the wall, brackets and all.

All eyes, including Bull's were on his enraged wife as she raised the gumball machine on high and brought it forcefully down upon her husband. Bull Smith collapsed in slow motion from his perch on the barstool. He slid to the deck, out cold. Gumballs from the broken machine rolled every which way across the dance floor.

Claudmantle, Holtel, and the others watched Bull's wife march across the tavern and out the door. They all left before Smith came to and the shore patrol arrived.

No one ever mentioned the incident to Bull later on the ship or any other place. Arthur Claudmantle would always remember the sight of Bull Smith out cold on the deck with the gumballs rolling crazily around him.

During the daily routine of a battleship at sea, the 4th division seamen were sent topside shortly after reveille to "turn to." On deck during the morning cleanup, we would take off our socks and shoes and with trousers rolled up to the knees, or in shorts, as the uniform of the day might dictate, grab the long-handled scrub brushes to scrub down the wooden deck. A coxswain or leading seaman would hose down with salt water as the sailors scrubbed in line. Good-natured Bruce Spaulding with his big wide feet, maybe, or smiling, cat-eyed Jack Frost from Louisiana Cajun country. Or Bob Roberts, Westley Potts, and Al Sandall from Illinois might lead the scrub down, handling the hoses and making sure we seamen did a proper job.

Down in the living compartments and other cleaning spaces, the profane cries of the compartment cleaners echoed through the ship.

"Wet deck. Goddamn it, get off the wet deck!" as they industriously swabbed the red linoleum decks around them.

Then the topside deck would be squeegeed to rid it of all the standing water, and finally it would be swabbed, or "clamped down." Other sailors would wash the paintwork with rags and buckets of fresh water to get rid of the salt-streaking of the seawater. Still others would tour the area with rags and brightwork polish, shining every piece of brass in sight. The teakwood of the deck would shine clean and white in the morning sun.

All of this activity took place before the call to breakfast at 0630. It was a refreshing exercise and served to get the deck clean and build up ravenous appetites as well. Then we would be served with hotcakes and bacon, bacon and eggs, or, if we were lucky, maybe S.O.S.*

On Fridays we would holystone the deck with a sand solution, sanding and polishing the wood clean with the long-handled sailor's tool. We would line up at arm's length to each other, starting at the center line of the deck. Then, in a sort of ballet, with sweeping motions back and forth, we moved the holystones, or sand stones, along the grain of the wood, our arms crossed over each other to grasp the handles and hold them steady. Steadily we moved backwards until we reached the side. Then we'd stand up straight for a few minutes to look out over the heaving sea, sparkling in the sun, laughing and talking as we looked over the side and fantail of the ship to see the great wide wake left behind us. It was a routine "field day" evolution.

When I first came into the division more than a year ago, the deck force was being run by a colorful first class boatswain's mate named Edmund Urbanski. He was regular navy, with years of China service to his credit, including a tour of duty in the U.S. gunboat Panay when it was sunk by Japanese planes in the Yangtze River in 1937.

*"Shit on a shingle"—ground-up hamburger on toast.

His broken English as he directed operations about the deck and, when he grew impatient, the choice expressions learned in ships and ports all over the world fascinated us. We'd never heard most of them before—at least I hadn't.

"Ski's great," Roberts said to me, laughing. "I don't know what he's talking about sometimes because he mumbles his words, but he's really something." I agreed.

Urbanski, whose thick-set body was covered with tattoos, kept his own personal wash bucket in the living compartment. It was nickel-plated and had his initials engraved on it. The handle was decorated with fancy coxcombing and a couple of Turk's heads and the salty Urbanski used to wash out his hats and socks and skivvies in it even though the ship had its own laundry. He did a better job, I noticed.

"Jeez, that's some kind of pail!" said a seaman who'd grown up milking cows. "Pail! You're not on the farm now, you shit kicker," a petty officer replied. "In the navy, it's a bucket."

The whole division admired the bucket but didn't dare touch it—or even go near it—for fear of arousing Urbanski's ire. Ski may have been good-natured enough most of the time, but this was one liberty he wouldn't permit. Hands off the bucket, a souvenir of China service.

When the *Oklahoma* entered port, all hands were ordered to shift into the uniform of the day—in Hawaii, it was skivvy shirts and shorts—and stand to quarters. Some of us in the deck divisions were assigned to handle the lines as the ship made her way to her assigned berth at a pair of quays next to Ford Island. Others in the 4th division would lower the accommodation ladder and swing out the boat boom as we came to our mooring.

"Look alive, Goddamn it," yelled Urbanski. "Get that Goddamn line over!"

All eyes would be upon us—from the sailors on the decks of ships nearby, to the high-ranking admirals and captains of the Pacific Fleet in their flagships and offices ashore. Any lack of smartness on the part of the Okie, whether it be in seamanship or the general appearance of the ship, would be mentioned later in the wardrooms and the bars in town.

"Get your asses moving, you buncha Goddamn landlubbers!" Urbanski, his hat pugnaciously squared down just above the eyes, seemed to be everywhere at once. "Sonofabitch!" Get that Goddamn ladder rigged out. Jesus Christ, you're supposed to be Goddamn sailors! Stupid half-assed kids. Sonofabitch. Can't you tie a Goddamn knot? Get that boom out or I'll kick your ass overboard."

Urbanski's voice bayed out across the harbor, his profanity practiced and polished, his threats to the seamen clearly understood. We admired his vocabulary. Of course there was nothing personal in any of it. Fellow seaman "Turk" Turcotte would look at me and laugh.

As soon as the division was secured, Urbanski would go below, take off his bos'n's pipe—the badge of authority he always wore around his neck—and change into a spick-and-span shore-going uniform, his mind on a few or more cold beers in town. His bulging middle was testimony to the thousands that had gone that way before.

24

A fter a time, Mullaley asked, "This trunk goes to where?" The reply sounded like Aldridge, "To topside; it's a long way down. We're sitting on the fourth deck. It's a long way."

"Can I see where it goes?" And Mullaley ducked under the water in the lower part of the trunk and, holding his breath, pulled himself down the ladder in the narrow escape hatch all the way to the main deck. There was nothing blocking his way! At least down the escape hatch.

He scraped the wood of the deck with his fingernails; he was sure it was the deck. Then Mullaley came back up inside the trunk and told a few of the sailors how far he'd gone. It was more than twenty feet down from where we were. I did not hear this where I was lying on the overhang or I might have acted differently.

"You're 180 degrees; it will take a lot to go out, across, and up; you've got to hold your breath all the way," Aldridge said. Some of us were not privy to this information either.

Actually, we were sitting or lying on a thirty-degree slant; we could feel the angle, but it didn't make much difference. For all intents and purposes, we were upside down and either sitting or lying on what had been the overhead.

The young Texan still wasn't sure of his way. Someone explained—it was Aldridge—how the ship was laid out. He should have told all of us, but he didn't. Hinsperger and I, and some of the men on the upper side of the trunk, did not hear this valuable information.

It would be hard enough for Mullaley to find his way up the trunk in the dark if the ship was right side up. But she wasn't.

"I'll go all the way this time," Mullaley said. Aldridge replied, "You shouldn't go unless you're determined to make it all the way." And, as sort of an afterthought, "We are all breathing the air and you will use it up."

Mullaley was skinny—he would try to make it down the escape hatch four decks, all underwater, across a good thirty-five feet of main deck, and then up to the harbor surface—another thirty feet at least.* Could he do it? He'd try. Mullaley was going down and out if he could— all the way.

"If you make it, tell them where we are," we said as he got ready to go. "Okay."

In just his shorts, Mullaley took a deep lungful of stuffy, smelly air, ducked underwater, and pulled himself down the ladder of the escape hatch.

"Make a straight line across the deck when you come out of the hatch," someone said.

Mullaley got all the way down, pulled himself through the hatch and, swimming on his back, pushed up against the deck. Like a huge crab, he thought, as he pushed and swam along. He couldn't see and hoped he was going in the right direction.

Then Mullaley hit the lifeline. He kicked around it—spun around— and went up fast through the water. Straining, he saw daylight as he got nearer the surface. Then . . . he was out! He'd made it! But it was impossible for him to return and let the rest of us know.

Mullaley figured he could have held on a few seconds longer—but that's all. Now he looked at what was around him there in the water. The *Arizona!* The oil was on fire! It was too much to take in all at once.

He was out! Almost three hours trapped down there and he was out. It was about 1100.

Mullaley was only in the water a short time, it seemed, when a motor launch came by and picked him up. The crew put a life jacket on the tired young sailor and put him on the up-turned bottom of the *Oklahoma*. He noticed that he didn't have his shoes on.

"Lie down and rest," the sailors told him. He did.

---

*Figuring that we were on the fourth deck down, then there were three deck spaces of more than seven feet each between us and the main deck, topside. The main deck, of course, was above water ordinarily, the water line being at about the second deck level. The harbor bottom was about forty-one feet from the surface where the *Oklahoma* was moored. When the ship capsized through the 150 degrees, the men in the handling room who had been about fifteen feet below the waterline, stayed at about the same depth as the ship spun around us—about 15 feet below the harbor surface. Therefore, it would be more than twenty feet down the escape hatch, a good thirty-five feet across the starboard side of the main deck, assuming a straight line to the side, more if not. And because the ship was resting at an angle—the starboard rail 30 degrees off the bottom —it would have been at least thirty feet more up to the surface. A total of eighty-five or ninety feet altogether. It was a long way to go underwater in absolute darkness under the most difficult of circumstances.

"Where are you from?" his rescuers asked. "How many are there down there?"

Mullaley told them what he knew.

After a while, a boat was called alongside and he was put into it to go across the harbor to the hospital ship *Solace*.

It was about noon.

The launch got to the *Solace* and Mullaley went aboard. There was a navy nurse there at the head of the gangway with scrambled eggs on her hat, he noticed.*

"Go wash," she told Mullaley. After he'd washed the oil out of his hair, a cook gave him some sauerkraut and weenies to eat.

25

Down below, we wondered. Had Mullaley made it out? Or was he hung up somewhere along the line? We had no way of knowing. If he made it, he'd tell somebody about us down here. If not . . .

After Mullaley had gone, no one said anything for a while. A few of us wondered if we could make it down the hatch. I just didn't know. Apparently, for various reasons, others didn't even consider it.

"Frig it! I'll never need this again," someone said, then threw a handful of change into the water. There was a splash.

The water continued to ooze into the trunk space from the handling room. A few of the sailors tried to break into the 5-inch magazine, then gave it up.† What for? It didn't go anywhere.

I said to Hinsperger, "Wimpy, if we don't get out of here, I'll bet you a dollar we'll suffocate before we drown."

"I'll take that bet," Hinsperger replied. "I think we'll drown first."

Silence. It was dark. Absolutely dark. I stared open-eyed into nothingness. All avenues of escape seemed closed to us. Except maybe the escape hatch below. I would have to try, but I wasn't quite ready to make that final effort. Not yet.

---

*Gold leaf on the visor indicated a rank of commander or above.

†Actually, unknown to us in the trunk, five men had been in the 5-inch magazine and had moved into the 5-inch handling room adjacent to the magazine when that area began to fill with water.

Popeye Schauf was thinking of his home back in Albany and of his father, who was a captain in the fire department there. At this time of year, when it got so cold and snowy, it was a dangerous job being a fireman in the big city, the capital of New York State. For that matter, it was dangerous anytime, but he thought that he might like to be a fireman too, when his hitch was up.

Now they were trapped in this terrible place. He knew he wasn't going to make it. I should have stayed in the CCC, he thought. He said a prayer.

Feeling a little warmer now that he had shed his water and oil-soaked clothes—everything except his skivvy shorts—was Frank Scott. He was aware of his friend, Pinky Davenport, sitting next to him even though he couldn't see him. Davenport wasn't moving.

"Is the hatch open to topside?" Scott asked.

"I'm going to find out. If it is, I'll swim out," Davenport replied.

"You've got to be sure and go the right way; we're tied up to the *Maryland*," Scott said. "Let me know if you go," he continued, "I'll go the same way, if I have to."

Scott's ears still hurt from the air pressure. He could hear something like Christmas trees burning, he thought. Christmas trees. What made him think of that?

He asked Davenport, "What is that, oil burning on the water?" His ears cracked.

"I don't know. I don't give a shit."

All that effort to get out, Scott thought, and then you'd just burn. How far was it to get out? How long would it take? Was it night or day? Would there be any room to swim between the two ships if they did get out?

Maybe they'd have to swim lengthwise along the ship and you couldn't hold your breath that long.

Scott was not alone in asking these questions of himself.

Scott turned to the boatswain's mate Red Aldridge, "How are we tipped?"

Aldridge replied, "What the hell's the difference? We're not going to get out anyway."

Scott wasn't ready to give up yet and, hearing this, almost went berserk. He went after Aldridge, there in the dark, looking for him to say it wasn't so. Every time he took a step, he'd bang his shins on a piece of metal. He couldn't get at Aldridge and cooled off after a bit. His shins hurt terribly and that helped to quiet him down, too.

Maybe I can still find a way out of here, he thought. But how? Maybe the bilge hatches. Where were they? There weren't any here. There's a small hatch; I can feel it. Scott tried to unscrew the nuts and finally got them off. But he couldn't see and gave up the effort. It didn't lead any- where, whatever its purpose.

Scott heard Davenport say, "When there's no more air, I'll swim out."

"Me too," Scott said. "Knock on the ship if you get out," he said to Pinky, "if it's above water—so I know."

He would check on Davenport every once in a while to see if he was still there.

Scott wondered if his friend, Francis Skifnes, whom he had been playing acey deucy with when all this started, had got back to his ship, the *Maryland*, okay.

And what about Harry Nichols from back home who was on board? He remembered how they had asked to be assigned to the *Oklahoma* be- cause of those large portholes in the stern—the ones they could get out through if the ship were sinking. Someone was trying to warn them way back then. He should have gone out right away; he was there sitting on his bunk, next to the porthole when the attack started. But no, he had to man his battle station like everyone else. And then Templeton threatened him with a gun! Jesus Christ. He should have stayed in the Iowa National Guard where he'd been a corporal. Nichols, too. And now it was too late.

It looked like Aldridge was right after all. They'd never make it out. But all this seemed hopelessly negative. There was no direction when there should have been.

Every once in a while, one of us in the trunk—it was probably Al- dridge who began—rapped out the distress call *SOS* . . . - - . . . in Morse code, with a dog wrench, on the steel bulkhead. The sound rever- berated through the surrounding area, a ghostly call for help from within the metal skin of the *Oklahoma*'s body.

Would it do any good, this metallic cry for help? Could anyone hear it? Would they try to rescue us?

"Maybe the Japs have taken over outside," someone said. "They'll never even try to get us out."

Even then, the faintest sort of hope that the navy would not let us down, would try to rescue us if they could, was part of our subconscious thinking. But we still could not acknowledge it in word or thought.

"We'll never get laid again," a sailor said sorrowfully from the upper part of the trunk, apparently thinking of the girls he'd had in half a dozen liberty ports.

What was going on out there, I wondered. We had no way of know- ing. All kinds of unpleasant possibilities occurred to us. A few of us had not given up thinking of escape as yet. Some of the few would make their individual attempts in the hours to come. We were tormented by our doubts.

Someone said to take off our skivvy shirts to make a lifeline for an escape down the hatch. Was it Roberts? It sounded like his voice, I thought. The men removed all their clothing except their shorts. I took mine off and handed it down to a sailor on the ladder below; I couldn't tell who it was. "Give me your skivvy shirt, Wimpy," and I handed his down, too.

The light was turned on for a moment or two so we could see. At least this seemed a positive move.

When he took off his trousers to help make the lifeline, Davenport turned to Scott and handed him a twenty-dollar bill he found in one of the pockets.

"Here, Scott, don't let anyone say I didn't give you anything." He continued, "Go over to the New Senator and enjoy yourself. Don't spend it all at one time."*

Sitting on the ladder, Scott took the bill, looked at it, felt it. He swore feelingly. "No one but you would think of something like that now," he muttered in disgust. "I'll take it right up to the corner and spend it." Then he tossed it into the water.

Davenport shook his head; he didn't think this was very polite of his friend, Scott.

Then all at once . . .

"I'm going to try and get out." Davenport took a deep gulp of the putrid air, ducked under water, and tried to make it down the escape hatch. He got as far as the main deck. He could feel the wood. But Davenport couldn't make himself leave what seemed to be the relative security of the escape hatch, which led back up inside the trunk to where his shipmates were, for the unknown dangers outside. Once he had left the hatch, he could never go back.

Davenport came back and tried again, going down for the second and last time. He couldn't go on and desperately made his way back up the hatch, his lungs bursting. "If I'm going to die, I might as well go back and die with the rest of them," he said to himself. And then he was with us again, wet and stinking from the oily water, gulping for air.

But yet, he never gave up hope. "We can hold out for a couple of days," Davenport was saying, mostly to himself. "The navy just has to get us out."

I was an interested observer to this effort by Davenport. I thought that if he didn't come back, I would give it a try. But he came back twice, unable to go all the way. I was discouraged. I would have to think about it some more. I didn't know what to do.

---

*A bawdy house, one of several in town frequented by men of the fleet after pay days. Others were the Congress and the Anchor. Three dollars per.

Time crawled by. I could see by the occasional flash of the light that the water was rising slowly, persistently pushing its way into the broken ship and our tiny corner of it. The body of a shipmate left behind in the handling room bobbed against the entrance to the trunk. It seemed as if he wanted to join the living there. Someone pushed the floating body away, behind some wreckage. There was nothing we could do for him now. Sooner or later, we might join him and the others there.

The taste and smell of fuel oil was sickening. More time went by. Water was still coming into the ship. I felt it; I didn't have to see or touch it. Ever so gently, it lapped insidiously into the trunk space, inch by inch.

Strangely, except for those in each man's immediate vicinity, we did not know who else was in the trunk, even though the space we were imprisoned in was small.

There was no coordinated effort at escape, as there should have been. It was true that each man's life was his to save, if he could, and he was entitled to try to do so in the best way he could, but the total effort would have been more successful if we had acted together under the guidance of a senior petty officer, sharing whatever information we obtained or knew of, so that all might benefit.

Each of us, however, was making his own effort to survive—either by acting or doing nothing—almost totally isolated from the others, even in the small area of the trunk space. It had been that way in the handling room during the last moments before the ship had capsized. Most of us were so taken up with our own survival during those few minutes that we did not necessarily notice the actions of another man or several men only a few feet from us. But this was natural in the emergency of the moment. The ship had rolled over fast and there was little time to act. Here in the trunk space, it was different—we had the time.

There was little conversation. What there was came in sporadic bursts, then silence reigned once more.

My watch had stopped. Time did not matter. I dropped it into the water with a splash. There goes Bill Water's secondhand watch I'd bought. Now I'm out the money and the watch. Had Waters made it out? It never occurred to me to look at the watch to see what time it stopped.

I took out a handful of change from the pocket of my shorts and dropped the coins into the water, one at a time, absent-mindedly listening to each tiny splash. Jesus Christ. How was I going to get out of here? Would I ever see daylight again?

I must have still had hopes, because I was careful to keep my folding money—the ten and the one—neatly folded in my wallet. Just in case.

No one said anything. Not even Hinsperger, next to me. What could they say, anyway? I lay back and stared into the darkness, seeing nothing, my mind wandering back over the past year or so since I'd first come to Hawaii, in time for Christmas, 1940.

Would we make it to another Christmas, now less than three weeks away? What was the date? Sunday, the 7th of December?

Last year at Christmas the navy had hosted some children from the area around Nanakuli, where a recreational center was maintained. I was there for a few days on R&R. There was entertainment and gifts and good cheer enough to last the year, almost. We sang carols and songs of the islands around a huge fire built on the beach, as the surf ran in and the stars shone down through the clear, dark night.

How different from the cold and snow of a New England winter. But not so different, really, for the Christmas spirit was the same around the world wherever people celebrated the birth of Christ.

The declaration of the national emergency in mid-1940 had resulted in the movement of the *Oklahoma* and the rest of the battleships, aircraft carriers, and most of the cruisers and destroyers from their West Coast home ports to the more forward position in the Hawaiian Islands in early 1941. The Pacific Fleet had remained here since then, secure in its protected anchorages in Pearl Harbor, going and coming on various exercises and maneuvers in neighboring waters. The Aloha Tower and Diamond Head became familiar landmarks; the anchorages off the city of Honolulu or Lahaina Roads hosted the *Oklahoma*.

The islands were beautiful—so different from my Massachusetts home. The sun shone, and the trade winds sighed in over the Waianae and Koolau mountain ranges of Oahu where rainbows were commonplace in the shower-covered peaks. The vegetation was lush: palm trees were everywhere and orchids and hibiscus grew wild or cultivated. Sugar cane and pineapple fields stretched out toward the higher elevations of the mountains behind Pearl Harbor.

We swam at Waikiki and were a bit disappointed in the lack of surf and narrow beach. We tested the waves at Nanakuli and Waianae and found them larger and more challenging on the windward side. We looked at Diamond Head and the Pali and took tours around the island with our cameras just as the tourists from the mainland did.

Perhaps we might stroll through the gardens of the Royal Hawaiian Hotel at Waikiki, where sailors were always welcome, and then attend a nearby movie. Or we might sit around in a tavern near the beach drinking a few beers and telling sea stories. Afterwards, we'd catch a bus back to town and wait for a bus in front of the Army and Navy "Y" with mobs of sailors from every ship in port, or share a faster taxi ride back to Pearl Harbor.

If we were not too broke, we might visit one of the local night spots where we would dance with the smiling girls of Oahu and, in ever in-creasing numbers, girls coming over from the mainland. The mixture of races in the islands was the richest I'd ever seen. Oriental—Chinese, Japanese, and Filipino. European—Scotch, English, French, and White Russian. American—the descendants of New England missionaries and whaleboat crews. And, the handsome native Hawaiian Islanders, whose Polynesian ancestors had come in their outrigger canoes from the islands many thousands of miles to the south.

I had met a pretty island girl one day not too long ago when walking up a winding, flower-bordered road. We dated each other occasionally whenever the *Oklahoma* was in. We danced, went to the movies, and swam under the stars. We talked of many things. I told her about my Yankee upbringing, what it was like scrubbing the *Oklahoma*'s decks, my dreams for the future. She told me about the islands, the customs of her people, how they lived and worked and played, her school and what she liked to study, and something of her own dreams.

We began spending more time at sea as the year wore on. I didn't mind because that was what I had joined the navy for—to go to sea.

Schauf and I stood lookout watches in a windowed enclosure atop the Okie's tripod mainmast. We could see the mighty battleships of the fleet in line astern, and Popeye thought that nobody was going to bother us as long as we had all those battlewagons with the great, huge guns. I looked and dreamed of how one day I would become a naval officer and, in time, an officer of the deck on the bridge of one of those great ships. Maybe even the captain of one some day far off in the future.

Schauf would bring me back to reality. We spent a good deal of our watch coughing as the pungent stack gases drifted back to choke us. "Christ, Young, we'll die up here!" Popeye complained.

It was a relief when the watch was over and we could descend the ladder to the safe broad deck below.

26

How do we get out of here? Through the voids? How? Mike Savarese was thinking of what he could do next.

A long time went by. Would he ever see Brooklyn again? The streets, the elevated, and the Brooklyn Bridge? At least he shouldn't have to pay for those smashed bowls up in the compartment now, he thought. Or down in the compartment, because up was down and down was up in this crazy, stinking place. Still, knowing the ways of the navy, he couldn't be sure about the bowls, even so. He wouldn't worry about it. Idly, he threw his money away and it splashed into the water.

Pinky Davenport, mindful of his bodily needs, even under these extreme circumstances, said, "I've got to take a crap."

"Well, don't do it in here!"

Needing to go to the head, but thoughtful of the others there in the trunk, Davenport left and found his way back into the half-flooded handling room. He was gone a few minutes, then he returned, the only sailor from our group to perform this otherwise normal function during our long hours of imprisonment—the only one I was aware of, anyway.

This seemed to bring matters back into perspective, for the time being.

The fun-loving and sometimes boisterous Davenport had acquired his colorful nickname after an interesting evening ashore in Honolulu. He had come back to the ship with a pair of ladies' pink panties stuck in the waistband of his trousers. Where had he been? How had he come by this souvenir of a Honolulu liberty? He didn't say. Tired, Davenport climbed into his bunk and went soundly to sleep without getting out of his liberty whites.

The mischievous Mike Savarese, noting that Davenport was out of uniform, so to speak, gently removed the offending garment and carefully draped the panties over the sleeping sailor's head. Davenport snored blissfully on.

When reveille sounded that morning, Davenport woke up to gaze through the filmy gauze of the panties and, thinking he was in some sort of pink netherworld, jumped out of his bunk in great alarm. We thought it was hilarious and the good-humored Davenport eventually saw the fun of it. He accused Savarese of doing this to him and of course Savarese denied any involvement.

Davenport was known forever afterward as "Pinky" to the sailors of the 4th division.

All at once, Popeye Schauf spoke up loudly, "Them Goddamn Japs! I just bought a new box of cigars! And they're gone! The whole friggin' box!"

"Oh, for crissake, Schauf! To hell with your stinkin' cigars!" someone said. "Is that all you can think about?"

It was. Popeye was really upset.

His voice turned to me. "I didn't just lose the box, Young, I left the cigar I was smoking on the angle iron around the barbette when I came inside. And that's gone, too! I was going to light it up again when I got out. Lousy, friggin' Japs!"

"Oh, forget it, Popeye, it doesn't make any difference," I told him. "Don't worry about it."

Savarese finally asked Roberts, "If none of the hatches are shut, it's clear all the way to the main deck. Then which way?"

Roberts replied, "Let's find out."

Then Savarese said, "If I go down, I can scrape the wooden deck with my fingernails. I can find out if it's clear all the way and come back and show you."

Tying the skivvy shirt lifeline that we had made around his waist, Savarese ducked underwater. I watched him go under. If he could make it down, so could I. I'd give it a try. I hoped he didn't get hung up on something and that he'd come back and let us know.

Savarese pulled himself down the ladder in the escape hatch until he could feel the coaming around the hatch at the main deck. He scratched the wooden deck like he said he would and came back up. The skivvy shirt lifeline got tangled up and broke away.

When he got back up, out of breath from his underwater exertions, Roberts shined the light on his fingernails so he could see if Savarese had gone all the way down. He had.

I was glad to see Savarese back.

The light was growing weaker and was shut off again.

"You're using up the air," Aldridge said.

"It's my air, too, Goddamn it!" Savarese replied, annoyed at the first class boatswain's mate.

Roberts said to Savarese, "You've got to figure twenty-one feet down, then you've got to swim out at least fifty feet over the deck, then up."

I didn't hear him. I don't think the others did either.

Savarese said, "Jesus, I barely made it back up here. It's a long way. How can I make it all the way?"

I wondered, too.

Savarese decided to go down a second time. He got all the way down to the last rung of the ladder and couldn't make himself let go. He came back up. "I can't make it."

I lay back on the overhang again. Getting out through the escape hatch looked to be impossible.

All of a sudden, big, awkward, nonathletic Dan Weissman spoke up, "Frig it. I'm going and I can't swim!"

We were surprised. "Go ahead," we said. I was sure he couldn't do it. But it was his decision to make. It was his life. We had no right to stop him at this point.

Weissman ducked underwater and didn't come back.

Did he make it? The question was in all our minds.

I thought of how we had been teasing him in the living compartment just before the attack. He was eager to go ashore . . . a girl on his mind.

Could this be why he had made his all-or-nothing attempt at escape despite the odds against him?

Dan Weissman did make it. He popped to the surface and was seen by Clarence Mullaley, who was still lying on the Okie's bottom. The courageous Weissman had become a man in another way. He told his rescuers that there were sailors trapped in the ship below, near no. 4 handling room, and that they were still alive. As best he could, the exhausted Weissman told them what the conditions were below. The crew had to help him into the boat. It was just about noon.

Just after Weissman had gone, Roberts told Savarese, "You've got to go down with one thought in mind. Let go of the hatch. Go all the way. There's no turning back. If you come back, it's to nothing. You've got to go with no thought of coming back."

Roberts's words were directed at himself as well as to Savarese. He hadn't tried himself yet. He added, "You go first and then I'll go."

"Balls!" Savarese said, who had made the effort twice. "You go first."

I waited too. If anyone could make it, Roberts could. I'd wait and see and then I'd try.

I lay back on the overhang, glancing below from time to time to see if Roberts had made up his mind. It was dark but I would be able to tell—a flash of the light, a gulp of air, a splash as he went under. I'd know. And if he didn't come back, then I'd go. Would I have the nerve to go all the way? I didn't know. I tried to make up my mind to make the try.

"Are you okay, Wimpy?" I asked.

"Yeah," he said drowsily. I realized the air was getting stuffy. We'd have to make it out of here pretty soon or the air would get too bad.

Roberts stood there in the water. A long time passed. He just stood there, looking down at the water that beckoned him down to its dark embrace.

Savarese tried a third time. Again he got down to the end of the escape hatch but couldn't force himself to go any farther. He came back up and sat on the ladder. "Forget it. If you want to go, go," he said to us. I decided to wait a while longer although I really didn't know why anymore, for I was not afraid. None of us could afford the luxury of fear by then. Whatever it was that held me back, I was not yet prepared to make my try.

For my friend Mike Savarese, the effort was over. People say you can see in the dark, he thought. It wasn't so.

Somebody tell us what to do. We're just young sailors but we'll give it a try . . .

Roberts had figured when they had made the safety line of skivvy shirts that it could guide a man back to the trunk if he found a way out.

Or maybe they could run some kind of communications line back in. It was stretching things a bit.*

But we had to do something, anything, to get out of here.

We were sitting or lying in the trunk in just our shorts. The water rose more and more as it seeped in from the handling room, which slanted off some feet below us with the list of the ship. Roberts made a mark on the bulkhead to make sure the water was rising, and after a while, the mark had disappeared. It was just a matter of time, he figured, until the water would rise over them to completely flood the area.

Roberts told the man next to him the water was rising and said not to say anything so as not to panic anyone. Most of us knew it anyway.

How long had we been sitting here? There was no way of knowing. The time of day—or night—didn't much matter at this point, only as it applied to how much time we had left before the air ran out and the water rose over us. How long would the air last? Maybe the Japanese had landed and taken over outside.

We were losing air, of that Roberts was certain. There must be a leak somewhere, causing the water to rise. In any event, the oxygen was being used up. And all they had was that one light, which could give out at any time. He finally made up his mind that he was going down the escape hatch and go all the way.

There was less air to breathe, and all those guys are rebreathing the same air, he thought. Pretty soon he'd grow too weak to do anything. It was now or never. He'd swim out or die trying. It took a lot of courage.

I don't think I can make it, the petty officer thought. There's not much chance the hatches are open all the way. But Savarese had said they were.

I hadn't heard Savarese say that, or I might have tried right then. When he came back up a couple of times, I was discouraged at making the attempt. There was an obvious lack of communication among us there in the trunk. Roberts went under twice. Each time he panicked and came up again. Then he figured that the same air he used in returning could take him the same distance farther on. He told the man next to him, "The next dive will be my last. I'm not coming back."

It was the hardest thing he ever did. He was just plain scared of dying, he realized, just as he had been back in the handling room when the ship began to list. He had been excited then; he couldn't afford to be now. He must have stood there in the water for an hour or more, it seemed, before he could force himself to go.

---

*But not that much. After the first men had escaped from the trunk, a diver released a buoy into the escape hatch. By this time, however, we had moved and there was no response.

All at once, he turned and carefully handed the light off to a sailor near him, quietly, so many of us did not see him go, and without a word, took a deep breath of air and slipped under the water. He started down the escape hatch, on his way. To life? Or death?

Roberts had the route set in his mind. Time was what counted. He felt that he could hold his breath for about two minutes. And, if he exerted himself too much, not that long.

Running through his mind as he pulled himself along the ladder was the thought, "I'm not going to make it, but I'm not coming back to the trunk!"

He kept his head, in any case, and figured he shouldn't swim down against the pressure of the water. He would grab hand holds on the rungs of the ladder and pull himself along as rapidly as he could.

He was about to give up when suddenly he popped out of the hatch. Then he lost his bearings. What direction should he go in? It was pitch black because of the depth and the oil on the surface, which blocked out any light at all. And he was in the giant shadow of the ship's hull which towered over him, supported by her superstructure and great tripod masts stuck in the mud on the harbor bottom.

Roberts tried to swim out from under the ship. The buoyancy of his body kept him pressed against the deck. He could feel he was getting nowhere.

Then he rolled over until he was upside down. Pushing himself away from the deck, he'd push up, then swim, push up, then swim . . . on his back, crabwise across the deck. He felt as if he were blacking out.

Suddenly he felt something scraping along his back. He began to panic. He was caught! But it was only the lifeline, and it was enough to snap him out of it, mentally. He kicked like mad to get clear.

Finally, he was free of the ship. He was sure it was the end of the line for him, however—that he'd never make it. His jaw was locked in a death grip. He wanted desperately to breathe.

He was going straight up now. He could feel it. But he couldn't seem to get anywhere. The water was passing by his face—he was conscious of it. He was swimming hard. The water streaming by his face felt as if it were going one hundred miles per hour. It was a strange sensation. Now the water was changing color!

God!

Roberts could see the surface above him. But he wasn't getting there. His limits had been reached long before. It felt as if his lungs were exchanging places with his stomach. Both lungs and stomach were in his throat. He hung on—it seemed like forever.

Then! He hit the surface, jumping out of the water like a huge porpoise. The air exploded out of his chest.

"Hooray! Oh, boy!" he yelled.

Westley Potts, in his motor launch, saw Roberts pop out of the water, "green as a frog," he thought. Where had he come from?

Roberts hollered and cheered to be alive. It was sort of funny, he thought, with all the destruction around him—burning ships—and here he was cheering away. But he had won his fight for survival.

A fifty-foot motor launch from the hospital ship *Solace* spotted him. The *Oklahoma*'s petty officer swam toward it. Then his arms went dead and he couldn't breathe.

Damn, he thought, I must have a touch of the bends. I can't swim! Roberts started to go down. The tremendous effort he'd made to escape that watery grave. Now this!

A sailor in the boat saw that he was in trouble and dived in after him. He held Roberts up until the boat came alongside.

The crew couldn't get him into the boat, he was so oily. Finally, a sailor knotted his fingers in Roberts's hair and jerked him out of the water into the boat. Roberts couldn't figure out how he did it. All sailors wore their hair short—navy regulations.

His rescuers wrapped him in a blanket and the engineer stuck a cigarette in his mouth . . . just like in the movies, Roberts thought. He could barely breathe! His chest felt as if it were in a vise. The damn cigarette was killing him! He struggled and coughed. The sailor finally understood and took it away.

"There's twenty guys trapped down there," Roberts told them.

The time was about 1300—1:30 in the afternoon. It didn't seem like five hours he'd been trapped in the ship.

Roberts climbed up the gangway of the *Solace*. Behind him was the upturned hull of the *Oklahoma*.

Sailors still lived inside her. How many would survive?

27

There were no more attempts at escape. It was too late. I had waited too long to make my try. I dared not now. It was stuffy in the trunk; the air was getting bad. None of us any longer had the strength, although we may not have realized it yet.

If we were to make it out now, rescue would have to come from the outside. Was any rescue effort being made? We had no way of knowing.

Perhaps if there had been stronger leadership on the part of the petty officers in the trunk, we could have made a coordinated effort to escape rather than acting individually or not at all.

Even then, all eleven of us might not have made it. But we would have been able to make a positive choice based on whatever information was available. That was the important thing. Maybe all of us could have made our way out during those first few hours. Maybe not. We'd never know.

Faced with what seemed a hopeless situation, we dreamed and dozed. The stale air dulled our senses.

It was quiet there in the trunk. Our faith would help us during the difficult hours ahead.

We prayed in silence. God, please get us out of this. Grant us a reprieve so that we may see our loved ones . . . sail away on another ship in more peaceful waters . . . see the sun and the sky and the stars again. Forgive us for our sins . . .

Once I heard the sound of gunfire rumbling down through the ship and water to reach us in the trunk.* No one paid much attention to it— there was nothing we could do. It came from another world, it seemed.

"Do you hear it, Wimpy?"

"Yeah, our AA in action."

"It's the Japs again," someone said.

After a while it was over.

"No more girls for us," a voice blurted out of the darkness.

I thought of pretty girls, laughing, full of life. I had to speak, "Damn it, I'm not even twenty years old and I'll never know or love a girl again."

My dreams seemed to be over—dreams as ill-defined as a kaleidoscope sometimes, colorful, shifting.

My dream of the navy came to me one day during a family picnic on the rocky tip of Cape Ann on the north shore of Massachusetts. The battleship *Mississippi*, I was told, or it might have been a heavy cruiser, had anchored off the picturesque town of Rockport. I watched the massive gray warship as she swung at anchor off the shore. I saw the colored signal flags and pennants run up and down the signal hoists and I had heard the ship's bell sound each half hour. Liberty launches had brought their happy cargoes of laughing, carefree sailors to the landing in the town. They swung off along the streets in their dress blue uniforms—in groups, or on the arms of pretty girls.

I was caught up in the high romance of the moment, and after I'd

---

*About 2300—11 P.M. Three planes from the carrier *Enterprise* came in for a landing on Ford Island and were shot down by mistake by nervous gunners.

graduated from high school I'd joined the navy with my parent's blessing, if not their enthusiasm. The recruiter told me I'd have to go to sea for a year—brush up on my physics, too—before I could apply for entrance to the Naval Academy.

I shivered a little in the cold dampness of the capsized *Oklahoma.*

The ocean was cold where I came from. On the nearby beaches the frigid waters of the North Atlantic pounded in against the shore. Salisbury, Seabrook, Hampton, Rye. The sun was hot on the sand, but the ocean water along the north shore of Massachusetts and the New Hampshire coast was so cold most of the time that only a New Englander could stand it.

I shivered again, there in the trunk. Each of us dreamed and dozed, in the dark, and no one heard.

Two or three sailors decided that they would see if the ship's Lucky Bag, which led off the trunk, would offer a better place for the eleven of us to stay.

Was it flooded? We didn't know. The door was closed, dogged down tight with steel dogs on either side.

It wouldn't take us anywhere, we knew that. The Lucky Bag had only one opening—that watertight door. The bulkheads were of solid steel, almost a quarter of an inch thick.

But we had to do something. The water was continuing to rise in the trunk and was coming up over the lower rungs of the ladder on which some of us sat. Those sitting there kept moving up the slant of the ladder, higher up along the list of the ship, in order to keep dry.

"We've got to test for air in there," someone said. Whoever had the battle lantern flicked it on. The light was weaker but I could see the door well enough from my place on the overhang. One of the guys opened the tiny airlock at the top of the door to see if the Lucky Bag was flooded. All eyes were riveted on the airlock to see if a jet of water came out at us. Nothing happened. Good. "It seems okay," someone said.

"Let's undog the door and go in."

"Okay, damn it, let's do it. It's the Lucky Bag. It's got to be more comfortable in there than where we are."

A couple of men undogged the door and swung it open.

"C'mon, Wimpy, let's go." I said.

Leaving our precarious perch on the steel platform, Hinsperger and I, along with the other nine who had been sitting or stretched out on the ladder below us, entered the Lucky Bag. The light just barely showed the way. But it was enough to see us into our new home.

We could see that the Lucky Bag apparently was dry. Thank heaven for that. There were peacoats and mattresses to lie on—plenty of them. We could stretch out on these.

Wearily, we sank down on the clothing and hammock mattresses and stretched out on the thirty-degree incline of the overhead. It was a dead end in here but it was more comfortable, for sure. The three bulkheads—after, port, and starboard—were without openings as was the deck above us and the overhead on which we lay.

The only way out was by the way we entered—through the water-tight door back into the trunk.

We left the door open and someone threw a couple of peacoats over the raised metal coaming along the bottom of the hatch so the water wouldn't seep in from the trunk. Every so often someone would check it. Although the water in the handling room and trunk space was still rising slowly, it wasn't coming into the Lucky Bag. Not yet.

Schauf and Hinsperger dozed off. Mike Savarese and I were over by the after bulkhead. Mike figured the best thing to do was go to sleep. He thought that if we were going to die here—and it seemed to him we were going to—then he'd just drift off into nothingness. It was the best way, he thought.

Pinky Davenport dozed off, too. He kept hoping although he didn't know why. He still felt he might last a couple of days, if he took it easy.

I had not given up as yet, but I had to admit our chances were not good—almost none—of getting out. I dared not hope, and yet I suppose I did, for a rescue attempt to be made, and if made, successful. Did they even know there were men alive down here? Could they conduct any sort of rescue effort considering what must have happened up above, and what might be going on right now? We did not know. How long could we hold on? For what? What would become of us?

Shortly after we entered the Lucky Bag and settled down with our thoughts, a voice spoke to me from out of nowhere. I sat up straight where I lay against the bulkhead. The voice came to me through its steel. Who was it? I strained to hear.

"Is anyone there?" it asked.

"Yes, yes, who are you?"

Our hopes were raised but as quickly dashed again.

The unknown voice told us, "There's some of us trapped in here in Radio IV. There's some guys trapped in Steering Aft right next to us, too." I didn't know it then, but Al Ellis was one, along with some of his fellow quartermasters.

"We're from no. 4 handling room," I shouted back. "We're trapped, too, here in the Lucky Bag. There's no way out!" I did most of the talking because I was closest to the sailors in Radio IV.

"We can't get out, either," came back to me. "Is there water in there?"

"In the turret. We're all right in the Lucky Bag. We have peacoats to lie on. It's dry here. But the water's rising. We're losing air. Do you know anything?" Mike and I were both talking.

"No, we're trapped in an air pocket," Radio IV replied. Two of the radiomen who had been talking to me identified themselves. "My name's Roiland," one said. "I'm Tom Hannon," said the other.

"Steve Young from the 4th division," I replied. "Is there any chance of someone trying to rescue us?"

"No, none that we know of. It looks bad. We're just sitting around in here. Same with steering aft. Can you see?"

"We have a light; we keep it turned off to save it."

"Let us know if you hear anything."

"Yeah, sure. You, too."

"Okay."

The conversation trailed off. At least the eleven of us in the Lucky Bag knew we had company down here; that others were trapped like us. It wasn't much to cheer us up at all. The guys in Radio IV were in as bad a spot as we were. I imagine they felt the same way.

"Quiet down. Don't use up the air." Aldridge again. Who else? Every so often, he or some one of us would rap out . . . - - . . . on the bulkhead with the dog wrench. S - O - S!

We lay back on our makeshift beds.

The hours drifted by and we dozed and dreamed and remembered. And prayed now and then.

The air was getting bad; it seemed to weigh down upon us. All I wore were my shorts. Most of the time I was warm enough, then I got cold and pulled some of the peacoats over me. And then I was warm again. It was a gradual, insidious thing that was creeping over us to take our consciousness away.

Davenport saw Frank Wood's face where he'd last seen him back in the carpenter shop. "Come on, Wood, let' go!" And the sailor's reply, "No, I've lived my life . . . "

"Some of you stay awake and let the others sleep," Aldridge said.

I lay back on the peacoats and dozed off.

28

I was growing weaker along with the other ten men in the Lucky Bag, although we were not consciously aware of this. It was bound to happen; the hours had taken their toll. The stresses and strains of those first violent minutes of concentrated action followed by the desperate but unsuccessful attempts to escape had worn us down mentally as well as physically. We had had nothing to eat or drink for almost a day, although we had no idea of time. I, for one, was neither hungry or thirsty. Our prison was damp as well as dark, and it reeked of oil. But I was comfortable enough, most of the time neither too cold nor too hot. Some of us got cold from time to time and covered ourselves with peacoats. Some perspired as the Lucky Bag got stuffy with rebreathed air and the heat of our bodies.

Water began to leak over the hatch coaming into the Lucky Bag from the adjacent trunk space. It began to collect in an ever-deepening pool in the lower end of the compartment. A few of us realized it, but we made no move to close the door. We needed as much air as possible and would have to risk the water coming in. Most of us were stretched out on the high side, anyway.

My mind drifted back to boot camp in Newport, late August 1940. I remembered the two fun-loving cooks who had gotten drunk one night in town—down at the Blue Moon Cafe on Thames Street. After rolling back to the training station over the Coasters Island causeway, they had decided it would be a good idea to take a bath—in one of the galley's large soup tureens. They had been caught by the masters-at-arms, singing and splashing away in the mist of their unauthorized nocturnal bathing. A court martial was convened the next morning and the cooks got fined, busted back to seamen, and shipped out to sea on one of the old fourstack destroyers that used to anchor off the city.* All within the hour. I never touched soup again during my stay in Newport. Where were the two cooks now?

There in Newport with me were the two boyhood friends I'd enlisted with, Herbert Jones and Warren Allen. Allen was in the cruiser *Helena*

---

*The first of the four-stackers would be turned over to the British in September 1940. Soon, fifty of these versatile ships would cross the Atlantic once again on their way to Britain in exchange for bases in the Caribbean. Bermuda and Newfoundland bases were granted outright. The destroyers would perform as gallantly on convoy duty in Britain's war against the German U-boats as they had in World War I.

tied up at 1010 dock. Was he okay? Jones was all right, back at North Island in San Diego.

They knew Slapikas and Savage too; we had been in the same company under the benevolent command of good old Chief Meadows, who got so mad at us one day that he threw his sword violently against the brick wall of Barracks *B* and broke the tip off. His raging temper was something to behold.

Savage and Slapikas—dead on the shell deck. If we hadn't been ordered below, maybe we'd all be out and probably still alive—at least off the ship. There was no use at all in blaming anyone. What was done, was done.

I could see the companies of white-uniformed sailors marching in review on the sloping, grass-covered parade ground in front of the Naval War College in Newport. There was the sparkling blue of Narragansett Bay. High atop the flagpole, the Stars and Stripes whipped in the same brisk breeze off the cool Atlantic that tugged at our neckerchiefs tucked under jumper collars. There were the two brass cannons, gleaming in the sun, the huge Rhode Island seagulls, and the frigate *Constellation,* a famous warship of another time.

The *Constellation* had been brought out of retirement and recommissioned by the navy to serve as a receiving ship for a new generation of navy men. We were part of the recommissioning ceremony. Her sails were not rigged and her gun ports would be forever silent, but her masts stood straight and tall, and her deck was firm beneath my feet as I went below to sling my hammock. She was my first ship, though only for a day or two, and I could sense the sailors of another day around me—those who had so valiantly served a young America.

And now, a century and a half later, these present-day platoons of sailors, looking so serious as they marched along, were immaculate—from round white hats set just so, to belt and khaki leggings over shining shoes. I was one of them. As far as I could tell, everyone was in step as the band blared forth with "Anchors Aweigh" and other naval marching songs. Pinpoints of sunlight flickered from the tips of bayoneted rifles carried at shoulder arms. There was Chief Meadows with his sword, out in front of Company 10.

"Ready! Eyes right!" There was the president, Franklin D. Roosevelt, and Navy Secretary Frank Knox; we could see them out of the corners of our eyes as we marched proudly past the reviewing stand, eyes alert and steps sharp.

The shiny brass of the cannon distorted our images as we passed. The flag of the president of the United States was flying at the yardarm. We would remember this day as long as we lived.

Ready! Eyes front!

What would happen to all the happy young sailors in that review? What would be their fate in the days to come? The faces I knew so well in those ranks of marching sailors—how many would be obscured by the clouds of war that blotted out the sun, enveloping them in a misty nothingness?

It was darker now as these young men marched off into the distance to their individual destinies . . . to navy schools, ships in the fleet, the *Oklahoma*. Their ranks had thinned, I could see, with this first terrible blow—would thin even more as they struggled and fought and died in the oceans of the world so that people everywhere could live in freedom and in peace.

The vision was very real to me lying there in the darkness. Those companies and platoons of ghostly white uniforms worn by men who were no more, who had ceased to be. I watched them as they marched jauntily off, hats squared and rifles on their shoulders, flags flying high, until earth met sky and they joined the others who had gone before them . . . from the *Ranger*, *Constitution*, the *Monitor*, and the *Maine*. I could see my own face and body there among them. There! Right there!

The vision faded. I seemed to wake from my reverie.

It couldn't be. President Roosevelt had assured our mothers that they need not worry, that they had not raised their sons to fight in foreign wars. This, he had promised fervently, they would never do.*

Damn it! Why did I have to die down here like this . . . trapped in a sunken ship? We were all alone—the eleven of us in the Lucky Bag, the guys in Radio IV and Steering Aft—cut off from the world outside. No one could see me or the others here; they could not know of our final torment.

If death had to come my way, why couldn't it have been up in the sun or under the stars, in the open air? On the deck of a ship while the guns were firing or charging the enemy on some foreign shore? That was the way it should have been.

But here in the darkness, imprisoned in our iron cell, without a chance to fight back. To defend ourselves. It wasn't fair. Death would come slowly to embrace us here. There should be something honorable and even romantic about dying for your country . . . if you had to die. Damn Japs. Could I meet the test? Still, perhaps to die like this required a special kind of courage . . . for all of us. I didn't know. Perhaps I was feeling sorry for myself. I'd have to hang on . . .

*While radios carried the fireside messages of assurance, convoys escorted by American warships were already operating in the North Atlantic, and as the year of 1941 ran on to its dramatic climax, U.S. destroyers engaged in an active, shooting "non-declared war" against Nazi U-boats.

My fists were clenched. Perspiration covered my forehead. Then slowly my anger subsided in the hopelessness of that place. I lay back once more on my bed of peacoats. "Oh, God," I prayed silently, "relieve us of our torment. If it is your will that we die here, then please watch over my family and comfort them. If I have sinned in your eyes, then forgive me."

Time moved on. The water rose slowly as the air leaked out of the air pocket that sustained us. It could not last much longer. I figured I'd win my bet with Hinsperger that we'd suffocate before we'd drown. But I wouldn't give up; I'd hang on as long as I could.

Would anyone come for us? Did anyone know we were here? Was rescue possible? I dared not think of it. The anxiety would have been too much for me.

My mind wandered off once again and I was back in New England with my family and friends. Then the dream faded.

Sometimes I was aware of my surroundings, as I think the others were, but as time wore on we lapsed for longer and longer periods into a sort of unconscious awareness—neither one or the other—in a state of limbo. We could still respond—most of us—but there was nothing to respond to there . . . no physical challenge for the moment. Because we were quiet and almost motionless on our beds of peacoats, we used less air and our hearts beat slower. With no oxygen-consuming, energy-sapping exertions on our part during the long night; we were able to sustain life a few more hours. Perhaps someone or something had willed it to be this way. But we were slipping into oblivion and soon it would be too late.

Wait . . . wait. Don't excite yourselves. Just a little longer.

I thought of many things. Or nothing at all.

I remembered the trip by train across the breadth of America to join the fleet in Long Beach Harbor. It was a great adventure; everything was new and interesting. It seemed like such a long time ago.

I had been both awed and thrilled when I'd seen the mighty warships of the Pacific Fleet at anchor off San Pedro. "Oklahoma!" the coxswain called, and those of us who were to join her crew got into the motor launch with our seabags and hammocks for the ride across the harbor to our new home afloat.

The huge gray battleship lay at anchor inside the breakwater, her tall tripod masts and massive superstructure dwarfing the cruisers and destroyers moored closer in to shore. Squatting silently on her decks were four great gun turrets, roots extending three decks down, the ten long steel fingers of the 14-inch guns pointing fore and aft. The first part of my dream had been realized, the dream I'd had that day off Rockport and Cape Ann when I'd seen my first great navy ship swinging to her anchor.

I had met new friends. Rudolph A. "Turk" Turcotte, from the town of Ware, Massachusetts. My mother's birthplace. Turk was a good sailor; he later requested a transfer to the Asiatic Fleet. It was granted and he left the ship. There was George "Whitey" Raskulimecz, a light-haired, smiling sailor from New Jersey. He became a favorite of Red Templeton. And Raymond Vidito from Lowell, Massachusetts, now striking for signalman.

Now dusk was falling over the harbor and as the sun slowly dipped below the horizon, the intriguing lights of Long Beach and San Pedro gradually blinked into view. Ships' bells sounded the hour and the changing of the watch, their ringing notes pealing across the water to be caught and echoed by each ship in turn as they moved along.

It was time for evening colors and the melodious notes of the bugle acknowledging the end of another day in the Pacific Fleet echoed and reverberated across the harbor to blend with buglers' calls to colors on dozens of other ships. We turned to face the national colors aft, saluting until they were lowered from the flagstaff to be folded and stowed away until 0800 of the new day before us.

As the last faint note died away, the red aircraft warning lights atop the masts and the white boat boom, gangway, and anchor lights winked on simultaneously. Friendly yellow light showed forth from portholes along ships' sides.

Small boats showed their red and green running lights as they crisscrossed the harbor. Dozens of oil derricks rising out of the water showed their own red warning lights.

Evening had come to the fleet in southern California.

All in all, it was rather a romantic scene to a young sailor venturing forth into the world. Where would I travel, what would happen to me in the days to come?

I could hear the music of "La Paloma" playing over the general announcing system, as it did every night before the movies started. The notes of this romantic Spanish melody seemed to be playing in the Lucky Bag where I lay. I opened my eyes; nothing. I closed my eyes again, to recapture the memory.

Now the notes of an Italian folk song played over the decks. "Amapola, my pretty little poppy . . ."

Time for the movies. Sailors in the duty section or who were not going ashore took their seats on mess benches brought up from below, or on no. 3 and 4 turret tops, to view the movie. A screen rigged on the main deck, aft, began to reflect the images of Clark Gable and Jimmy Cagney, Lana Turner and Betty Grable. I fell in love with Claudette Colbert and admired the adventurous Victor McLaglen.

After the movies, the 4th division unrigged the screen and swept down the area. Benches were removed and we went below to turn in our bunks. First call sounded and five minutes later the plaintive notes of taps wafted along the weather decks and into each living compartment in the ship.

Following the shrill of the bos'n's pipe, the word was passed, "Now all hands, keep silence about the decks." We drifted off to sleep.

I could almost see and hear the misty form of the bugler sounding taps as I lay here in the darkness on the bottom of Pearl Harbor. It was the final call of the day and he was blowing it especially for us.

The face began to blur; then it was gone. It was dark.

PART 5

Out of the Darkness

29

Suddenly, out of the darkness, a hammering sound . . . in short bursts, then longer . . . automatic.

The noise of it reverberated along the steel decks and bulkheads. It was some distance from us. Where? How far?

Startled out of my semiconscious dreams, I woke instantly, my eyes wide open though I couldn't see. I sat up straight on my bed of peacoats.

What was it? What was that noise? My mind tried desperately to identify it. My heart pounded in my chest. I caught my breath.

It stopped as suddenly as it began. As suddenly, it started again. Had I imagined it? I waited for it to start again. Would it? I strained with the tension of hearing something unexpected.

"What is it?" someone asked off to the left of me.

"Maybe the Japs are trying to torture us," someone replied.

"Yeah, they're letting water in so we can sink all the way," one of the others said.

That didn't make sense at all. "No, no," I said. "It's something else. Listen."

Then . . . the metallic rapping began again. There was no mistaking it. But it was farther away this time. It stopped. We waited. Long minutes went by. Nothing more. More time. It seemed a long time.

What was going on?

Christ Almighty!

Was it possible? Were rescuers looking for us . . . trying to get us out of here? SOS! . . . . - - . . . The dog wrench pounded on the bulkhead. We're here! Here in the Lucky Bag!

Did we dare hope again? We could not speak of it just yet. It was too much.

Why did the hammering stop, then start again, farther away, then stop once more?*

My body was rigid with suspense. I dared not hope but I couldn't help it.

More minutes passed. A long time.

Again! The hammering was louder now. Someone spoke the unsaid

---

*Rescuers were finding their way down through the part of the hull that was above the waterline with their pneumatic air hammers, through the double bottom into the void spaces, and farther on, to make contact with those of us trapped below.

thoughts of all of us. "They're trying to get to us! To cut us out! They're using an air hammer!"

It was almost too much for us to grasp. To be snatched from almost certain death . . . to live again . . . was more than we were capable of fully understanding just then.

The strain was almost unbearable. My eyes were wide open though I could see nothing; my ears strained for the slightest noise though I could hear nothing for the moment; my mouth was open to breathe in the rancid air my pounding heart demanded.

There it was again! More hammering! Persistent . . . demanding in its urgency. I could feel it as well as hear.*

S - O - S! S - O - S! . . . - - - . . . banged the dog hammer to let them know where we were.

A sailor began to get excited, panicky, there in the middle of the Lucky Bag, somewhere in the dark. I didn't recognize the voice.

"Get us out! Come get us out of here! God help us!"

It was understandable, but this we didn't need just then. The rest of us realized that to lose control now would help none of us.

"Shut up! Quiet down!" I said to whoever was making the racket.

"I'll bang you over the head with the dog wrench, if you don't stop," someone else threatened.

The sailor got himself in hand and stopped. Despite the suspense, he was the only one to get overly excited—and then just for a few seconds.

Then Popeye Schauf began to sound off under the strain. His friend Davenport threatened to throttle him and he quieted down.

I shouted through the bulkhead to the guys in Radio IV. The noise seemed to be coming from that direction. I put my hands on the thickness of steel that was between us.

"What's happening?"

"They're trying to get us out!" the men in Radio IV yelled back to us. "They're coming after us!"

"Tell them we're in here!"

"Okay! Don't worry! If they can get to us, we'll tell 'em!"

My eyes turned toward the sound of the air hammer. It rapped and banged. Closer, it seemed.

---

*Rescue efforts began as early as 0930, 7 December, but the real effort to free us began sometime after 0100 on 8 December when sailors from the *Oklahoma* and other ships and civilian workers from the navy yard brought air compressors, pumps, chipping tools, and torches alongside the part of the hull still above water. It would still be some time before those trapped in the Lucky Bag, Radio IV, Steering Aft, and the 5-inch powder handling room could hear their efforts to free them. We had no knowledge that any attempt at rescue was even being made until the first sounds of the air hammer were heard as dawn came over the islands.

None of us thought to close the watertight door to the trunk space even though the water was slowly running in over the coaming into the lower end of the Lucky Bag. What for?

We'd know shortly.

Suddenly, we heard the rescuers break through to the six men in Radio IV.* We could hear the radiomen shout with relief, heard them leaving their prison. I cheered silently. Now come get us!

"There's some guys trapped in there . . . in the Lucky Bag. Right there," I heard them say.

"We'll get 'em," a calm voice assured them from the other side of the bulkhead. I could hear the thumping and banging of men and equipment.

A great light of hope renewed came flooding over the eleven of us in the Lucky Bag. They were coming for us! We would be saved from this terrible place. We would live again!

The Lucky Bag was appropriately named, for sure. I hoped.

30

"Can you stand a hole through the bulkhead? We'll drill a small one through," a voice called through the quarter-inch steel to us.

Someone switched on the battle lantern. The light was dim.

"Hell, yes!" we shouted back. "Go ahead and drill, for Christ's sake! Hurry up and get us out of here!"

"Take it easy boys; we'll get you. How is it, is it dry in there? Any water? Just one of you do the talking."

"A little. It's okay. Go ahead!" I called to them.

The rescuers drilled a hole through the after bulkhead in the upper end of the compartment—about a quarter-inch in diameter, it seemed—only inches from where I was. My right knee was kneeling on the overhead, my left leg was stretched out and down with the list of the ship. I hung on to an angle iron that stuck out from the bulkhead.

"Are you okay in there!"

"Yes, we're all right," I replied. "Please hurry!"

As the head of the pneumatic drill withdrew, we heard a violent hiss-

---

*They were civilian navy yard workers in charge of Leadingman Caulker and Chipper Julio De Castro. Time was about 0800.

ing of air in the Lucky Bag. What was causing it? Why the hissing noise?

Water began to rise more rapidly over the feet and up the legs of the men in the lower end of the compartment.

"Hurry up! Burn us out!" someone shouted. "The water's coming up!"

The voice from the other side, so close but miles away, replied, "We can't. You'd suffocate in there."*

"Jesus, we'll drown if you don't. The water's coming up to our knees," a sailor shouted in the lower end. As yet, the water had not reached up to me.

"Calm down, boys; we're going to get you out. We're going to use a chipping hammer and cut a hole through the bulkhead. Take it easy."

The hissing of air continued. No one appreciated the significance. All eyes were directed at the tiny hole in the bulkhead. Would we make it, I wondered? The question must have been in everyone's mind. It would be close.

Suddenly, "Jesus Christ, the door! Water's coming in the door!"

All eyes turned toward the watertight door we hadn't thought necessary to close, the one leading to the partially flooded trunk and handling room.

The light was bad, but we could see that water was beginning to flood into the Lucky Bag in a torrent.

Thank heaven Red Aldridge had kept telling us to put out the light to conserve the battle lantern's batteries. We would have been lost without it. He'd also kept up his banging with the dog wrench to guide our rescuers and keep us from using up too much air. Though he hadn't provided much of anything positive in the way of leadership, he had most definitely contributed to the cause.

"Close the Goddamn door!" a sailor yelled. Some of the guys close by got over to it, splashing in the water pouring into the compartment.

The sudden reduction in air presure in the air pocket caused by the hole the workers had drilled in the bulkhead was allowing the water to come in and flood the area—we were well below the harbor surface. Air was escaping from that tiny hole! The sudden reduction in air pressure. It didn't seem possible, a tiny hole like that.

If we had thought of it, someone could have stuck a finger over the hole and stopped the air from leaking out until we got the door closed.

But no one did.

With a terrible racket, the chipping hammer powered by an air compressor began to pound and cut a horizontal slash in the steel.

---

*De Castro kept talking to us, trying to calm us down and reassure us. And probably himself, too, as he and his crew worked against time and the constant dangers they encountered on their side of the bulkhead, which was also well below the waterline. Actually, we kept ourselves under pretty good control during the hour or so it took to cut a hole in the bulkhead. As De Castro said later, "They never complained."

Three or four men were still trying to shut the heavy hatch door. Mike Savarese, who had been next to me near the bulkhead during the past few hours, managed to scurry across the compartment to help out. I stayed where I was so that I could help the rescue operation going on in front of me in whatever way I could, which didn't seem to be much of anything at all except to keep them advised of what was happening in the Lucky Bag and to encourage them to speed.

The men at the door saw now that the reason they couldn't get the door closed was that the peacoats were still draped over the coaming. They threw them off.

Sailors splashed frantically around in the water; we could barely see; I kept looking over at the door and could see water coming in fast.

Close the door again, now that the peacoats were out of the way. It was unbelievable the way the water was pouring in, the pressure building up against the door. "Hurry up! Get that fucking door closed!" someone yelled.

On the other side of the Lucky Bag, the chipping hammer dug its way along the steel bulkhead, powered by an air compressor that I hoped would not fail its users. It was slow going, cutting through the tough metal.

"The water's coming in fast through the hatch from the trunk," I informed our rescuers on the other side of the bulkhead. "We're trying to get the door closed."

"You'll be okay. Get it closed if you can. We'll get to you as fast as possible."

Savarese and a couple of guys got the two dogs pulled down at the top of the door—or bottom as we were upside down—and then the two dogs pulled up at the bottom.

But the middle dogs on the side were reversed and they couldn't spin them around to fully close the door. Water from the trunk pushed hard against them, spraying in each side of the metal door because it couldn't be properly seated.

The dogs—would they hold? Or would they snap off?

Jesus Christ, were we going to drown in here like rats at the very moment rescue was at hand? After all we'd been through?

They didn't dare release the top and bottom dogs again in order to open the door and free the middle dogs so they could secure them properly. They'd never be able to shut any of them then. The pressure of the water would be too great to push the door closed.

Damn it! Why don't they make those sons of bitching things so they don't spin around like that?

The men at the door had done all they could in those few seconds. Now it was up to the rescuers on the other side of the bulkhead to cut through to us.

So close . . . but a lifetime away.

Every one of us, on both sides of that steel bulkhead, knew it would be close, a race against time. Would the workers be able to cut a hole in the bulkhead before the water flooded over us?

Would we win or lose the race?

The chipping hammer pounded its way slowly along, cutting through the quarter-inch steel. Fascinated, I anxiously watched its progress. There was plenty of noise in the Lucky Bag now, where an hour before there had been only a deathly silence.

The air hammer rapped its way along the cut in the steel, chipping away at the toughness of the metal; air continued to escape the Lucky Bag in a great hissing sound, and the rushing, splashing noise of the incoming water filled our ears. I looked over at the door and saw water gushing in on either side. In the dim light of the battle lantern, it looked as if the door were bowing inward.

Would the door hold?

"Hurry up, for Christ's sake; the water's coming up to our waists!" a sailor yelled in the lower end of the Lucky Bag.

It was beginning to creep up my feet and legs.

"Keep your heads, fellows. Just do what I tell you. We'll make it!" from the man in charge on the other side of the bulkhead, in Radio IV.

We quieted down.

"Okay, but hurry!" I said. "Some of us are hanging on the overhead."

The chisel at the end of the chipping hammer made its agonizingly slow progress across the top of what would be a rectangular opening a few feet square—just big enough to squeeze through.

Now the hammer began to cut its way down one side of the square. I could see that we would be barely able to fit through the opening. Eleven pairs of eyes urged the chipping hammer along.

The water continued to rise. The door was almost covered. Sailors below me were in water up to their waists and chests now.

It was over my knees and rising.

We edged up higher, up the list of the overhead-deck, hanging on to angle irons and whatever else we could grasp. I hung on with one hand, making room for someone else to come up beside me. I got hold of somebody with my left hand and helped to pull him up out of the water. I don't know who he was.

We were hypnotized, our eyes concentrated on the chipping hammer and its slow progress as it cut its way through the metal. Now it began its third cut, along the bottom of the square.

Hurry! Hurry! Before it's too late. God, the water's coming up higher and higher. Faster. We were as high in the compartment as we could go.

The water was almost up to the level of the bottom cut that the chipping hammer was making. There. Three of the sides were cut through.

"Keep calm; hold on a little longer!" someone said. Julio De Castro, who was talking to us from the next compartment, helped us almost as much by his calm and reassuring manner as he did the pneumatic hammer.

Now the fourth side. The hammer stopped and retreated. Our fingers grasped at the metal to pull it back with our bare hands.

Right now, the difference between life and death was to get that piece of steel bent back so we could get out.

"Look out for your hands, boys. We're going to use a sledge hammer."

So close, yet he was a world away, separated by a quarter of an inch of steel.

The sledge hammer rang against the metal. The three-sided piece of steel bent a little. Again. And again. It just missed Scott's fingers.

"Don't use your hands!"

Gradually, the steel was pushed back; the opening widened as the water pushed at us from behind. Now the hole was open, just wide enough for us to scrape through!

It was just in time. The water was up to our chests and shoulders, flooding faster and faster into the Lucky Bag.

31

"Okay! Come on out of there. One at a time. Easy!" Our friend in the next compartment didn't have to tell us a second time.

Mike Savarese and I were the first two out because of our position next to the bulkhead. I was hanging on to an angle iron just above the hole and when Mike started through, my arm caught him in the throat, "Glug!" and he couldn't move. Not a bottleneck now!

It would have been funny if we weren't so pressed for time.

"Look out, for crissake," Mike choked. "I'm going out."

Anxious as I was to make my own exit, I couldn't keep back a grin. I moved my arm back.

"Come on, Mike, out!" I said.

Savarese ducked through the opening and put a foot down to touch the deck on the other side. He couldn't. So he brought his foot back inside the Lucky Bag and went out with both feet at once this time and hit the deck on the other side. He looked up to see daylight above him.

We urged him on; we weren't out of the woods yet. The flooding waters behind us pushed us forward.

I went out head first without bothering about my feet. Friendly hands on the other side reached out to grab me. Water from the Lucky Bag spilled through the hold as I came out.

I was out! Free! Alive!

I'd made it, after all.

"Up on my back, boy," a big Hawaiian grinned.* I had never been so glad to see a friendly smile in all my nineteen and a half years.

I smiled back. "Thanks," I said, "I'm okay."

He boosted me up out of the Radio IV compartment into a void space just above, and then I made it on my own to come up and out on the bottom of the ship to join my friend Savarese. We looked at each other and grinned. What could we say? It was good to be out and alive. Thank God.

Pinky Davenport came out slowly. "Are you afraid to come out of there?" a worker kidded.

"No, I'm taking my time; I'm enjoying it," Pinky replied.

Frank Scott saw Red Aldridge go through the hole, one of the first men out, he noted. Not quite the first; Mike and I were two who beat him out. The others followed, one by one, in an orderly fashion. But quickly. The door was holding but they were coming out with the water. Then the eleventh man was out and that was it. All of us who had gone through that long night below in Pearl Harbor had made it.

One of the workers offered to help Scott, and he told him, "You did enough for me; I'll make it by myself up to the next opening."

But he couldn't. It was eight or ten feet up and he was covered with oil as we all were, more or less.

"Here, step up on my shoulders; I'll help you." Scott was a bit hysterical with the relief of being safely out. "Here, step on my hands, then my shoulders." The navy yard worker boosted Scott up into a void space above. He walked the twenty or so feet that we all had walked and stuck his head up through the bottom.

The air smelled fresh and the sun was shining. He cried.

Popeye Schauf; Wimpy Hinsperger; Comin' and Goins; Eslick; Tillman, the electrician's mate; and the musician, Engen . . . we stood on the Oklahoma's bottom, oil covered and almost naked. It didn't matter.

We were all out! We were alive! It was a miracle!

Sailors on the battleship Maryland alongside the capsized Okie who had been watching the rescue operations cheered as the eleven of us came up out of the darkness into the sunlight. Davenport and I waved

---

*Navy yard worker Joe Bulgo from Maui, one of De Castro's team.

back at them and grinned. The survivors from the Lucky Bag and Radio IV before them were among the very few to be brought out so far from inside the ship of the more than four hundred officers and men who had gone down with the *Oklahoma*. There would be a few more, including Al Ellis and his fellow quartermasters from steering room aft.

It was 0900, Monday, 8 December. We had been trapped below for over a day—twenty-five hours. We could hardly believe it.*

A motor launch from the hospital ship *Solace* came alongside the bottom. We began to go aboard.

An officer asked Savarese how he felt. "Okay," he replied. He didn't ask me, but it didn't matter. A sailor gave us oranges and cigarettes. Scott ate his orange, peel and all. I peeled mine. The juice of the first food we'd had since hotcakes over a day ago was the sweetest I'd ever had.

Mike couldn't light his cigarette, his hand was shaking so. A sailor helped him, then reached over and lit mine too. I took a deep drag and coughed. But the tobacco tasted almost as good as the orange.

Savarese looked around at the destruction in the harbor and said, "It looks like we lost the war."

"Put out the cigarettes," an officer said. "There's oil around here." He was certainly correct in this and we sailors looked at each other and shrugged our shoulders while rolling our eyes up in the air. It sounded like we were home again.†

There were a number of other officers and men present on the Okie's

---

*The official records show the time as 1100, or two hours later. The author remembers it clearly as 0900, however, and that hour would be more in line with the time it took between the rescue of the men in Radio IV at 0800 and those in the Lucky Bag. The result was the same in any case.

†Leadingman De Castro and his men carried out a dangerous and masterful rescue mission, with De Castro providing the on-the-job leadership necessary to rescue thirty-two *Oklahoma* sailors trapped below in the ship. Many navy personnel were also involved in one way or another, from the *Oklahoma's* first lieutenant, Lieutenant Commander W. A. Hobby, Jr.; the engineer officer, Lieutenant Commander W. L. Benson; and Warrant Boatswain A. M. Bothne; to the hospital ship *Solace's* Cox. Joseph Hydrusko. Credit must go to them as well. But it was De Castro and his crew who were most directly involved in freeing us. De Castro received a commendation from the Commandant, 14th Naval District, for his efforts.

Following the rescue of the men in Radio IV and the Lucky Bag, De Castro, Bulgo, and the rest of the navy yard team went on to rescue the sailors trapped in the 5-inch handling room; steering room, aft; and the forward air compressor room, to make the thirty-two brought out alive. Two others were lost in an earlier rescue attempt when they were suffocated in the gas and fumes in the evaporator pump room.

When De Castro got back to his shop in the navy yard, after more then twenty-seven hours of back-breaking and dangerous work, someone came up to him waving an overtime slip, saying, "Why didn't you fill this out?" "Christamighty!" said De Castro. There was no transportation available, and he had to walk the five miles home through darkened streets.

upturned hull who were taking part in the rescue effort or as interested spectators. I recognized several from the *Oklahoma*.

Captain Bode, the *Oklahoma*'s commanding officer, who had been ashore during the attack, was nowhere to be seen.

And nowhere did I see our division officer, Mr. Rommel. Or his assistant, Mr. Spitler. It was strange they were not there if they had made it out okay.*

Standing up the upturned hull, I gazed around me. It was the same world I had left over a day ago, but as I looked at the smoke and wreckage of battle all around Pearl Harbor, I knew that life would never be the same again—for me, or for any of us. Like America, we had left our youth behind.

As I stepped into the *Solace*'s boat, I looked down a last time at the ship I had lived in, the ship I and the others with me had come so close to dying in . . . the tomb of friends and shipmates who were gone forever.

The mighty *Oklahoma* was no more. The flag, the colored signal pennants would never fly again. The ship's bell had rung its last half hour. Her guns were silent; her turrets full of water and lifeless men. How strange that in all her life she had never fired them at an enemy.

The launch moved out across the harbor, past the sunken *West Virginia* and the still smoking wreckage of the *Arizona*. The shock of what we saw was almost too much to understand in those first few minutes. It would take time to realize the enormity of what had happened.

I turned to look back at the capsized *Oklahoma*. We were the lucky ones, I knew.

I thanked God for giving us another chance at life. Out of the darkness and into the sunlight of a new beginning. I looked away from the and smoke we were leaving behind us. Overhead the sun was shining. Here and there fluffy white clouds passed along the blue of the sky. The early morning trade wind caressed our tired oil-covered bodies.

I looked up at the mountains behind the harbor, up to where the rain clouds touched the mountain tops. And I saw a rainbow there.

Ahead was the large red cross on the *Solace*'s high white side.

I turned to Wimpy Hinsperger and grinned at him. "Put away the buck for a souvenir, Wimp. Neither of us won that bet, thank God."

We walked up the accommodation ladder and the doctors asked us what was wrong with us . . . it was hard to tell under all that oil. "Nothing. We're okay," we all replied. We were given medically prescribed bourbon and coffee.

"I don't drink coffee," Davenport said. And he got a double shot as we all laughed.

---

*The captain and both officers were alive and well.

"I'm surprised they didn't just give us APCs, like they do for every-thing else," I said.*

"Who the frig's got a cigar?" Schauf asked. A corpsman got one for him. The rest of us punched playfully at the grinning Popeye as we walked away down the passageways into the ship to shower and get the oil cleaned off, back in our world again.

Davenport felt his beard and it felt as if it had grown out an inch during the time we'd been trapped in the bottom of the battleship *Oklahoma*. He'd have to shave, he thought.

*An aspirin compound.

Postscript

The Salvage and Loss of the *Oklahoma*

The navy decided to salvage the *Oklahoma*, mainly to clear the anchorage, for she was too severely damaged ever to go to sea again.

The salvage effort was a major one, involving the use of winches installed on Ford Island. Wire cables were run from the winches to the capsized ship, and she was gradually rolled back through her list of 150 degrees to an upright position. Divers pumped her out, removed the remains of approximately four hundred sailors who had gone down with her, and patched her up so she could enter dry dock. This was accomplished in December 1943, more than two years after she had capsized.

The *Oklahoma* was stripped of her guns and machinery and sold for scrap in December 1946, when the war was over and most of her surviving sailors had gone home to the villages and farms and cities of America. It was five years after the five Japanese aerial torpedoes had torn her side apart. She brought a sum of $46,000.

Tugs towed the hulk of the once proud battleship to sea, on their way back to the States . . . to make razor blades out of her as the sailors say. A tug got her five hundred miles out.

But the *Oklahoma* was tired, the life had been drained out of her, the seamen who had manned her were dead or gone to other, newer ships. They had taken their revenge on the Imperial Japanese Navy. The aircraft carriers that brought destruction to the U.S. Fleet at Pearl Harbor were gone themselves with their planes and most of the pilots who had flown them. It was all over.

Gradually, for no reason that could be determined, for the weather was good and the seas calm, the *Oklahoma* took on a list. The same port list she'd taken five years before. The list grew steadily worse during the next four days and the tug received permission to tow her back to Pearl.

But the *Oklahoma* would have none of this, either, and suddenly one night, when the seas ran smooth and the stars looked down, she unaccountably straightened up. She held herself high for a few moments, then sank straight down, taking a towline with her but not the tug. Just like that, no noise, no fuss, four hundred miles at sea.

Was this the way it was meant to be? Could the men on the tug detect a faint cheering in the air as if a thousand sailors and more were saying, "Good for you, *Oklahoma*! Go down at sea, in deep water, as you should, under the stars. No razor blades for you. They can make 'em from the Japanese ships and planes that did you in. So long, *Oklahoma*! You were a good ship!"

What Happened to the Men of Turret No. 4?

The *Oklahoma* lost 448 officers and men at Pearl Harbor. Of the men of turret no. 4, thirteen were killed in action 7 December 1941. Six men from the turret were rescued from the capsized ship.

Special note should be made that during his thirty-five-year naval career Captain Rommel commanded five ships, four destroyers, and a replenishment ship. Included in his decorations is a Bronze Star for combat while commanding a destroyer during the Korean War.

Referring to the attack on Pearl Harbor and the sinking of the *Oklahoma*, his first ship, Captain (then Ensign) Rommel said to me: "I have always regretted not having told the sailors I left behind in the turret to abandon ship."

The Crew of Turret No. 4, 7 December 1941*

Herbert F. Rommel, Ens USNR
4th Division Officer

Joseph C. Spitler, Ens USNR
Assistant 4th Division Officer

1. Aldridge, Willard H.	Sea 1c	Killed in Action (K.I.A.)
2. Arickx, Leon	Sea 1c	K.I.A.
3. Athas, Marion H.	Sea 1c	Bldg. 71, Ordnance Supplies
4. Beck, Edgar B.	GM 2c	USS *Louisville*
5. Bergstrom, Royal E.	Sea 2c	USS *Honolulu*

*Captain Herbert F. Rommel, USN. Courtesy USS *Oklahoma* Association.

6.	Brosky, Stanley	Sea 1c	USS *Helena*
7.	Brown, Alvin L.	Sea 1c	USS *Helm*
8.	Brown, Maurice M.	CTC	USS *Honolulu*
9.	Claudmantle, Arthur, Jr.	BM 2c	USS *Salt Lake City*
10.	Davenport, Russell M.	Sea 1c	USS *Honolulu*
11.	Easley, Herschel	Sea 1c	USS *Jarvis*
12.	Gunning, Everett G.	Sea 2c	USS *San Francisco*
13.	Hall, Jupert P.	Sea 2c	K.I.A.
14.	Hamlin, Dale R.	GM 3c	K.I.A.
15.	Hinsperger, Wilbur T.	Sea 2c	USS *Honolulu*
16.	Holzhauer, James W.	Sea 1c	K.I.A.
17.	Ingram, Darrell L.	Cox	USS *Hull*
18.	Johnson, Harold E.	Sea 2c	USS *Worden*
19.	Jones, Stanton E.	Sea 1c	USS *Helena*
20.	Krames, Edward C.	Sea 1c	USS *Helena*
21.	Kyser, D. T.	Sea 2c	K.I.A.
22.	Leonardi, Lewis F.	Sea 2c	USS *Hull*
23.	Lewis, Robert J.	Sea 2c	USS *San Francisco*
24.	Little, Philip E.	AS	USS *Hull*
25.	Miller, Jack V.	Sea 1c	USS *Worden*
26.	Moran, George A.	GM 3c	USS *Gridley*
27.	Mullaley, Clarence J.	Sea 1c	USS *Honolulu*
28.	McDowell, John R.	GM 3c	USS *Helena*
29.	McQuay, Clayton W.	TC 1c	USS *Helena*
30.	Nance, Rufus F.	BM 2c	USS *Enterprise*
31.	Oleson, Harald R. A.	TC 1c	USS *Helena*
32.	Potts, Westley F.	BM 2c	Com NYd Capt. Bode
33.	Raymond, Glenn H.	Sea 1c	USS *Northampton*
34.	Roberts, Howard E., Jr.	Cox	USS *Tennessee*
35.	Roesch, Harold W.	Sea 1c	K.I.A.
36.	Sandall, Albert F.	Cox	Mine Def. Adm. Bldg.
37.	Savage, Lyal J.	Sea 1c	K.I.A.
38.	Savarese, Michael J.	Sea 1c	USS *Honolulu*
39.	Schauf, William P.	Sea 2c	USS *Honolulu*
40.	Schultz, Clyde I.	Sea 1c	USS *Ellet*
41.	Scott, Frank H.	Sea 1c	USS *Honolulu*
42.	Shoemake, Edward C.	Sea 1c	USS *Hull*
43.	Slapikas, Edward F.	Sea 1c	K.I.A.
44.	Sonntag, Melvin F.	Sea 1c	USS *Hull*
45.	Spangler, Maurice V.	Sea 1c	K.I.A.
46.	Spaulding, Albert B.	Cox	USS *Louisville*
47.	Stallings, James E.	Sea 2c	USS *Pruitt*
48.	Stapleton, Kirby R.	Sea 1c	K.I.A.

49. Templeton, Louis C.	BM 1c	Bishop Pt.
50. Weissman, Daniel	Sea 1c	USS *Tucker*
51. Waters, William W.	Sea 1c	USS *Helena*
52. Whitman, Richard F.	GM 2c	USS *Helena*
53. Wiley, Norman E.	Sea 1c	Dispensary, Main Bks
54. Wood, Frank	Sea 2c	K.I.A.
55. Wortham, John L.	GM 2c	K.I.A.
56. Young, Stephen B.	Sea 1c	USS *Honolulu*

Hull Rescue from Capsized *Oklahoma**

DECEMBER 8TH
0800 From Compartment D-57½ (Radio IV)

Thatcher, G. J.	Sea 1c	
Roberts, N. O.	Sea 1c	
Roiland, H. S.	Sea 1c	
Cymerman, R. A.	Sea 1c	
Smith, M. R.	RM 3c	
Hannon, T. F.	Sea 1c	6 men

1100 From Compartment D-57 (Lucky Bag)

Goins, S.	Sea 1c	
Eslick, E. W.	Sea 2c	
Tillman, R. L.	EM 2c	
Aldridge, K.	BM 1c	
Schauf, W. P.	Sea 1c	
Young, S. B.	Sea 1c	
Scott, F. H.	Sea 1c	
Davenport, R. M.	Sea 1c	
Savarese, M. J.	Sea 1c	
Hinsperger, W. T.	Sea 2c	
Engen, J. K.	Mus 1c	11 men

1400 From Compartment D-25-M (5-inch Handling Room)

West, R. D.	Mus 1c	
Crenshaw, B. W.	Y 2c	
Harrelson, H. W.	F 2c	
Pittman, D. L.	Sea 2c	
Russell, C. E.	Sea 2c	5 men

1600 From Compartment D-63 (Steering Room, Aft)

Artley, R. L.	Sea 1c

*From the report of W. M. Hobby, Jr., LtCdr USN. Courtesy USS *Oklahoma* Association.

1600 From Compartment D-63 (Steering Room, Aft)—continued

Beal, W. A.	Sea 1c	
Jones, G. L.	Sea 1c	
Bounds, J. C.	Sea 1c	
Ellis, A. L.	Sea 1c	
Kennedy, H. S.	QM 3c	
Thesman, I. S.	EM 1c	
DeLong, G. A.	Sea 1c	8 men

DECEMBER 9TH
0230 From Compartment A-23-1

Staff, W. F.	CM 2c	
Centers, J. P.	MM 2c	2 men
	Total	32 men

Some of the men of the *Oklahoma*'s 4th division stayed in military service to retirement and should be recognized. Among them are:

Howard Aldridge, Chief Boatswain's Mate, USN
Edgar B. Beck, Chief Warrant Officer (Gunner), USN
Royal E. Bergstrom, Chief Boatswain's Mate, USN
Arthur Claudmantle, Jr., Chief Boatswain's Mate, USN, Chief Warrant Officer, USAF, U.S. Army. (Two tours in Vietnam)
Clayton W. McQuay, Chief Gunner's Mate, USN
Clarence J. Mullaley, Senior Chief Gunner's Mate, USN
Rufus F. Nance, Chief Warrant Officer (Boatswain), USN
Howard E. Roberts, Jr., Chief Boatswain's Mate, USN
Herbert F. Rommel, Captain, USN
Louis C. Templeton, Chief Warrant Officer (Boatswain), USN
Joseph C. Spitler, Captain, USN
James E. Stallings, USN, Master Sergeant, USAF

Killed in Action 7 December 1941

FROM TURRET NO. 4
Willard H. Aldridge, Seaman First Class
Leon Arickx, Seaman First Class
Jupert P. Hall, Seaman Second Class
Dale R. Hamlin, Gunner's Mate Third Class
James W. Holzhauer, Seaman First Class
D. T. Kyser, Seaman Second Class
Harold W. Roesch, Seaman First Class
Lyal J. Savage, Seaman First Class
Edward F. Slapikas, Seaman First Class

Maurice V. Spangler, Seaman First Class
Kirby R. Stapleton, Seaman First Class
Frank Wood, Seaman Second Class
John L. Wortham, Gunner's Mate Second Class

FROM THE 4TH DIVISION:
Layton T. Banks, Coxswain

FROM THE S DIVISION:
Harry E. Nichols, Storekeeper Third Class

Killed in Later Action during World World II

Edward C. Krames, Seaman First Class, USS *Helena*, 5 July 1943. (Battle of Kula Gulf)
Stanley Brosky, Seaman First Class, USS *Helena*, 5 July 1943. (Battle of Kula Gulf)
Herschel Easley, Seaman First Class, USS *Jarvis*, 9 August 1942. (Off Guadalcanal)
Harald R. A. Oleson, Turret Captain First Class, USS *Birmingham*, 24 October 1944. (Battle of Leyte Gulf)
William E. Walker, Boatswain's Mate Second Class, USS *Enterprise*, 24 August 1942. (A Japanese plane crashed into Walker's gun mount during the Battle of the Eastern Solomons.)

DIED OF INJURIES:
Albert Bruce Spaulding, Coxswain, USS *Louisville*, August 1942. (Died of injuries received in an accident in Kodiak, Alaska, returning to the United States in the *Honolulu*.)

ALSO KILLED DURING WORLD WAR II:
Thomas F. Hannon, Seaman First Class

Captain Howard D. "King" Bode of the *Oklahoma* went on to command the heavy cruiser *Chicago*. During the Battle of Savo Island off Guadalcanal, 9 August 1942, he took his ship away from the scene of the main action, in which three American cruisers and one Australian cruiser were sunk by an aggressive and victorious Japanese cruiser-destroyer force.* This unfortunate captain, whose actions were severely and justifiably criticized by his seniors and juniors alike, took his own life not long afterward, as much a casualty of the war as any who went down in the *Oklahoma* or in the four cruisers at Savo Island.

Special note should also be made of Turret Captain First Class Harald R. A. Oleson, U.S. Navy.

*USS *Quincy, Vincennes,* and *Astoria;* HMAS *Canberra.*

He died as he had lived—as a man—in the hard-fought campaign to retake the Philippines. All five feet plus of him.

His ship, the cruiser *Birmingham*, had come alongside the aircraft carrier *Princeton*, which had been badly damaged by Japanese air attacks, to help put out the fires that raged on board the stricken ship. Oleson could have stayed inside his gun mount, no. 3, but he came out to fight the fire. An explosion blasted along the deck and blew off both his legs.

He was conscious to the end and drank a cup of coffee while he joked with the sailors in the mount, "When I get my new legs, I'll get them long enough to reach the accelerator on the Cadillac I'm going to buy."

Then Oleson lay over on the deck and died. It was 24 October 1944, the first day of the Battle of Leyte Gulf.

After this brave sailor had gone back inside the turret that Sunday morning in December to warn his shipmates to abandon ship, when he might have gone over the side and left them behind as others had done, he either rescued or assisted in the rescue of at least three men from the 4th division and one from the 3d.

"I thought you couldn't swim," they said.

"I couldn't, but I learned fast," Oleson grinned.

Certainly, if any of the officers and men of the 4th division could be called a "hero," when mostly there were no heroes—only survivors— then Oleson would be one. But he would have laughed at the thought. To Turret Captain Oley Oleson, who had to stretch his way to get into the navy, he was just doing his job.

To the best of my knowledge, Oleson was never awarded a medal or commendation for his life-saving efforts on 7 December 1941, a day when many acts of bravery went unnoticed.

Congressional Medal of Honor, Ensign Flaherty and Seaman Ward*

FRANCIS C. FLAHERTY, Ensign, U.S. Naval Reserve
Citation: For conspicuous devotion to duty and extraordinary courage and complete disregard of his own life, above and beyond the call of duty, during the attack on the Fleet in Pearl Harbor, by Japanese forces on 7 December 1941. When it was seen that the U.S.S. *Oklahoma* was going to capsize and the order was given to abandon ship, Ensign Flaherty remained in a turret, holding a flashlight so the remainder of the turret crew could see to escape, thereby sacrificing his own life.

JAMES RICHARD WARD, Seaman First Class, U.S. Navy
Citation: For conspicuous devotion to duty, extraordinary courage

*Courtesy USS *Oklahoma* Association.

and complete disregard of his own life, above and beyond the call of duty, during the attack on the Fleet in Pearl Harbor by Japanese forces on 7 December 1941. When it was seen that the U.S.S. *Oklahoma* was going to capsize and the order was given to abandon ship, Ward remained in a turret holding a flashlight so the remainder of the turret crew would see to escape, thereby sacrificing his own life.

Navy and Marine Corps Medal, Chaplain Schmitt*

The citation below is in explanation of the Navy and Marine Corps Medal awarded posthumously to Lieutenant (junior grade) Aloysius H. Schmitt, Chaplain Corps, U.S. Navy.

One can only wonder why the navy did not see fit to grant Lieutenant (jg) Schmitt a much higher award, for he gave his life so that others might live, the highest sacrifice an individual can make.

> *Citation:* For distinguished heroism and sublime devotion to his fellow man while aboard the U.S.S. *Oklahoma* during attack on the United States Pacific Fleet in Pearl Harbor by enemy Japanese forces on December 7, 1941. When that vessel capsized and he became entrapped, along with other members of the crew, in a compartment where only a small porthole provided outlet for escape, Lieutenant (junior grade) Schmitt, with unselfish disregard for his own plight assisted his shipmates through the aperture. When they, in turn, were in process of rescuing him and his body became tightly wedged in the narrow opening, he, realizing that other men had come into the compartment looking for a way out, insisted that he be pushed back into the ship so that they might leave. Calmly urging them on with a pronouncement of his blessing, he remained behind while they crawled out to safety. His magnanimous courage and self-sacrifice were in keeping with the highest traditions of the United States Naval Service. He gallantly gave up his life for his country.

*23 October 1942, citation from Frank Knox, Secretary of the Navy, for the President. Courtesy USS *Oklahoma* Association.

Appendixes

Appendices

APPENDIX A
Plans of the *Oklahoma*

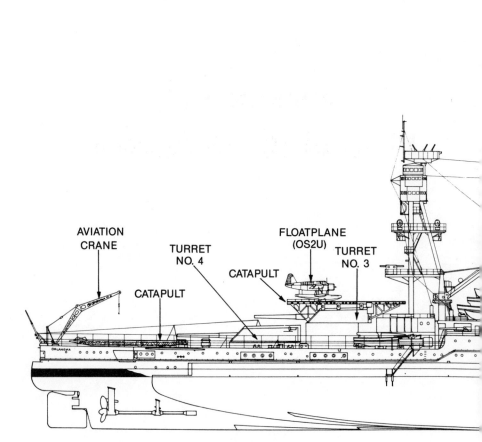

Fig. A-1. Outboard profile. From a drawing by A. D. Baker III in Norman Friedman, *U.S. Battleships* (Annapolis, Md.: Naval Institute Press, 1985), 200.

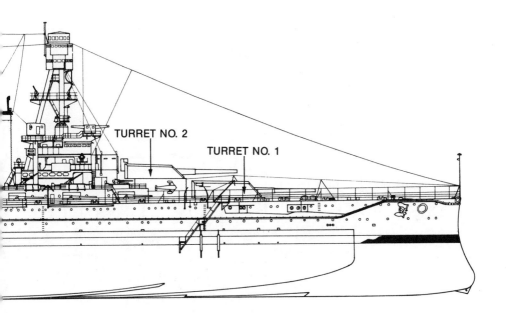

TURRET NO. 2

TURRET NO. 1

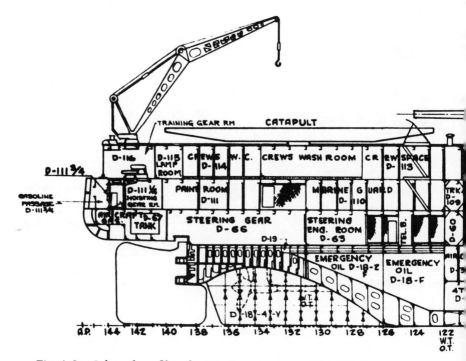

Fig. A-2. Inboard profile, aft. U.S. Navy, courtesy USS *Oklahoma* Association.

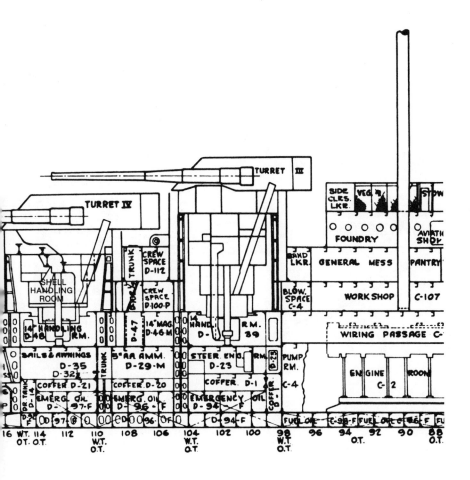

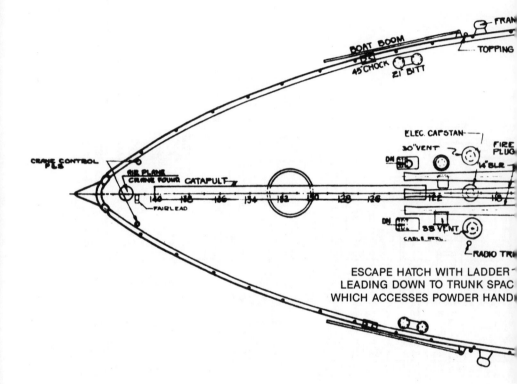

Fig. A-3.   Main deck, aft. U.S. Navy, courtesy USS *Oklahoma* Association.

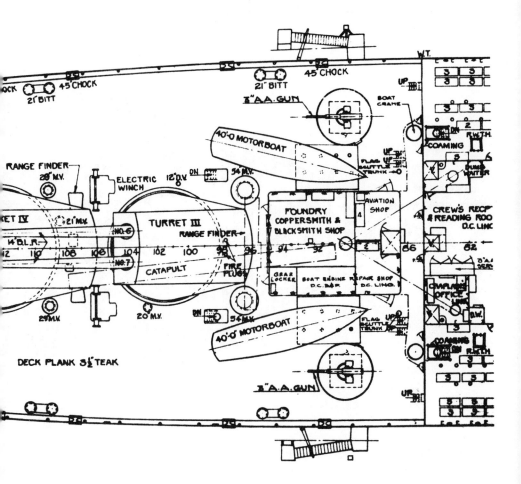

DECK PLANK 3½" TEAK

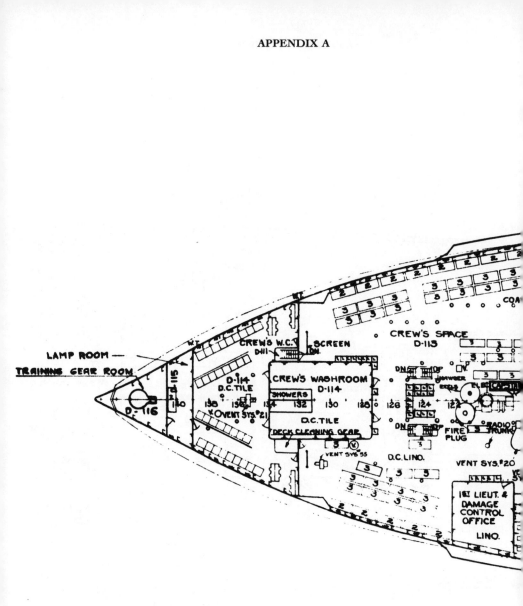

Fig. A-4.   Second deck, aft. U.S. Navy, courtesy USS *Oklahoma*
Association.

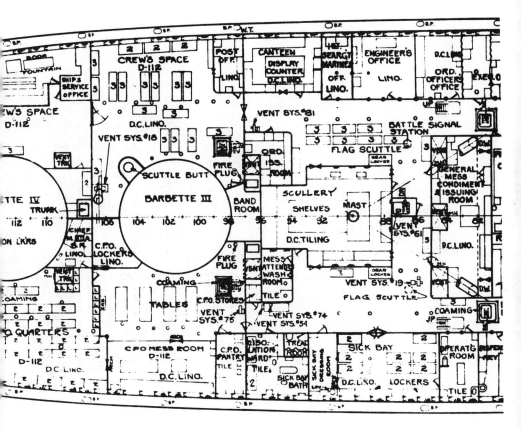

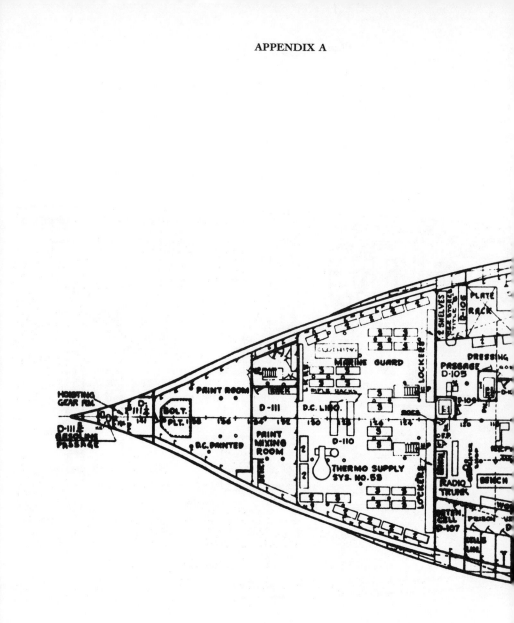

Fig. A-5. Third deck, aft. U.S. Navy, courtesy USS *Oklahoma* Association.

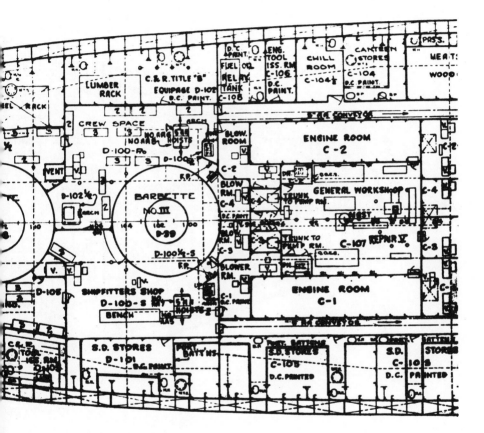

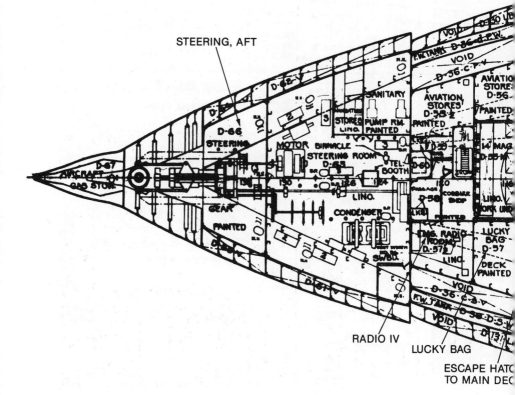

Fig. A-6. First platform deck, aft. U.S. Navy, courtesy USS *Oklahoma* Association.

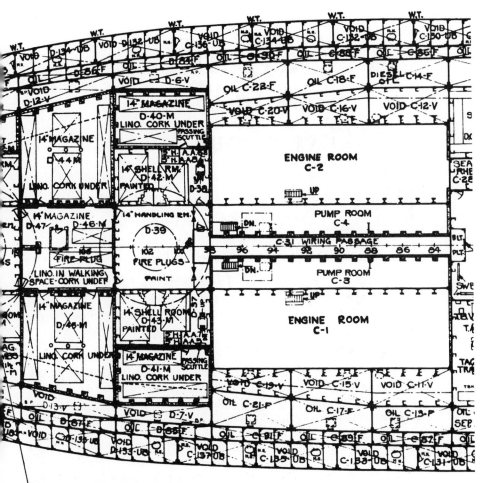

LOWER POWDER HANDLING ROOM
FOR TURRET NO. 4

NK SPACE WITH LADDER
CESSING TURRET NO. 4

APPENDIX B
A 14-inch, Three-Gun Turret

The description which follows applies generally to all modern turrets, 8-inch to 16-inch inclusive.*

Major structural subdivisions (see fig. B-1).

(a) **THE BARBETTE** is a cylinder of heavy armor surrounding the turret structure from the lowest protective deck up to the armored turret proper. The barbette is stationary and is not joined to the rest of the turret.

(b) **THE TURRET FOUNDATION** is a heavy structure of girders and beams built into the structure of the ship. It is cylindrical in shape and extends upward close to the inner surface of the barbette, to a point near the top of the barbette. At its top it supports the circular roller path, carrying the rollers on which the entire revolving portion of the turret rotates.

(c) **THE TURRET PROPER** is the heavily armored box-like structure from which the guns protrude, and which may be seen to rotate from the outside. The circular barbette armor extends from a point just below the armor secured to the revolving portion of the turret, down to the lowest protective deck of the ship, so that the turret roof, front, and side plates, together with the barbette and protective deck armor afford protection to the guns and machinery within the turret and to the magazines beneath the turret.

---

*From chapter 9, "Naval Gun Mounts," *Naval Ordnance* (Annapolis, Md.: United States Naval Institute, 1939), 220–22.

(d) **THE REVOLVING TURRET STRUCTURE** is all of the inner structure forming one assemblage with the turret proper and extending downward within the turret foundation to the deck of the lower powder handling room. The weight of this structure and the turret proper rest and rotate on the rollers on the roller path. All the operating compartments, machinery, and other gear are in the turret revolving structure and turret proper.

Interior subdivisions

(a) **THE TURRET CHAMBER** is that part of the turret surrounding the gun positions. It includes the gun chambers and the gun pits. The gun breeches are in the gun chambers, as well as the delivery ends of the shell hoists and powder supply. It is here that the guns are loaded.

(b) **THE TURRET BOOTH**, at the rear of the turret proper, is separated from the turret chamber by flame-proof bulkheads, and is so designed as to give the turret officer a direct view of the guns through suitable dead lights. Access to the turret chamber is obtained through doors. Each turret booth has a quick-acting lever or other device for operating the sprinkling system in the turret chamber and also in upper and lower powder-handling rooms and to drench powder in the train between lower and upper handling rooms. The turret booth is also fitted with a lever or other device for operating an emergency alarm. The turret booth is habitually-occupied by the turret officer when the turret is in operation.

(c) **THE HANDLING ROOMS** are spaces which are habitually utilized in the ammunition supply train for transferring powder or shell from the stowage to the supply hoists, from one hoist to another, or from one means of supply to another means of supply. These may be further distinguished as powder-handling rooms and shell-handling rooms. Shell stowage is the term used to designate open spaces where shells are stowed within the turret barbette on the circle decks at various heights and throughout the turret structure.

The magazines and lower powder handling room are adjacent to the bottom of the turret revolving structure. They are not in the turret proper but form an essential part of the ammunition supply facilities.

(d) **OTHER SPACES** are the storage battery room, training gear room, hand passing platforms (for powder), tank compartment for the sprinkler water tanks, blower rooms, etc.

Special apparatus

The general requirements regarding turret construction require that nothing shall be attached to the turret armor except fittings required by the structure, or fittings which by their nature and use cannot otherwise be placed for the efficient operation of the turret. Means are provided to prevent bolts, nuts, rivet heads, etc., flying in the turret as the result of shell impact. In all turrets, except single-slide turrets, flame-proof bulkheads separate the several guns.

A gun spray is installed near the breech of each gun and fitted with a quick-acting valve controlled from the turret booth, turret overhang, and gun chamber. Another water spray is fitted on the end of a flexible hose capable of being used in the gun breech or any other part of the turret gun chamber.

Each gun in the turret is fitted with a gas expelling device. Blowers are installed in the turret for ventilating purposes, and during gun firing the turret is maintained under a slight air pressure.

The intakes of the turret ventilating system are so located as to minimize the possibility of drawing into the system gases from fires in action. Care is taken, so far as practicable, to keep water and spray from entering the turrets through the gun ports, and sighting slits, while the turrets are being operated.

A sprinkling system is installed to drench powder in the gun chambers, upper handling room, lower handling room, and the powder train between upper and lower handling rooms where exposed in case of fire. Voice tubes, bells, buzzers, telephone, and fire-control instruments are installed.

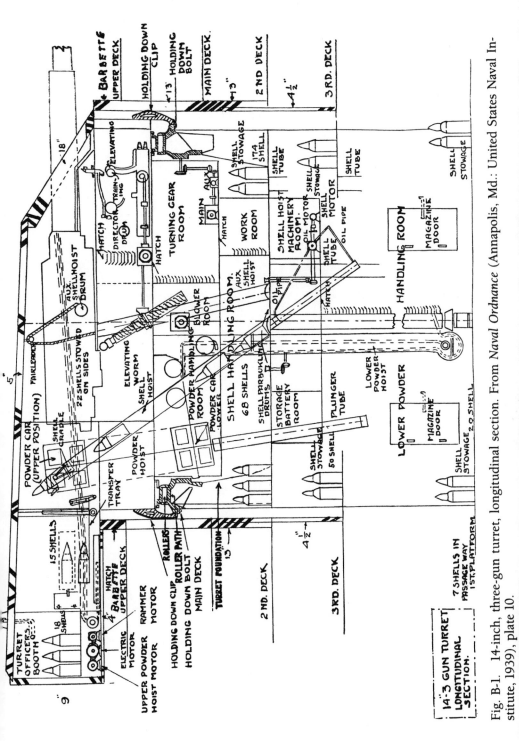

Fig. B-1. 14-inch, three-gun turret, longitudinal section. From *Naval Ordnance* (Annapolis, Md.: United States Naval Institute, 1939), plate 10.

Note on Sources

I first wrote of my experience in *Oklahoma* as she capsized and sank in the early minutes of the Japanese attack on Pearl Harbor in the December 1966 issue of the U.S. Naval Institute *Proceedings*. I knew then that I should expand my own story into the collective account of the sixty-some officers and men of turret no. 4 and certain others in the crew whose stories would be invaluable in such an account.

It was not easy to put the story together after all these years. Admiral Samuel Eliot Morison, the noted naval historian and Pulitzer-prize-winning Harvard professor, helped get me started more than twenty years ago. And through the years since then I was fortunate to have the invaluable assistance of navy people such as a former shipmate, the late Quartermaster Gerald M. "Dutch" Foreman, the *Oklahoma* Association's historian, who came up with addresses, lists, ship photos, schematics, and other aids.

This project would have been impossible had not the majority of the no. 4 turret crew responded to my inquiries in various ways—by letter, telephone, and in personal interviews—over the years. My thanks to all of them for furnishing their own experiences as the ship went down to settle in the mud of Pearl Harbor. I was even able to obtain photos of the time from most of them. Photographs were provided by the individuals pictured unless otherwise noted.

Sometimes my contacts with Pearl Harbor participants were surprising, such as one evening in 1987 in San Jose, California, at an *Oklahoma* reunion. I was introduced to the man whose shoulders I had stepped on as I evacuated the sunken battleship. Joseph Bulgo, Sr., a civilian navy yard worker at the time of the Pearl Harbor raid, was then living in San Francisco, after many years in his native Maui, and was the guest of honor at the dinner that evening. Ill at the time, he died several months later.

As I put the pieces of the puzzle together, matching individual accounts with each other, verifying and reverifying the action, I saw that my memory served me well. My own experience had made an indelible mark on my mind, of course, and in the days and months immediately following the Pearl Harbor attack, turret no. 4 shipmates who served with me in the Pacific campaigns told me what had happened to them as well. I have even checked out the sometimes quite colorful "sea stories."

In reporting the events of that morning of 7 December 1941, the cumulative memories of the crew of gun turret no. 4, my own included, have been a team effort, much as we had functioned as a turret crew many years ago. Some are gone now to wherever sailors are homeported. They too have contributed to the accuracy of this story.

The following individuals generously contributed their stories through letters, telephone interviews, and personal interviews.

NAME	RANK/RATE 7 DEC 1941	PRESENT HOME
Marion H. Athas	Seaman 1st Class	Eldora, IA
*Royal E. Bergstrom	Seaman 2d Class	San Diego, CA
Arthur Claudmantle, Jr.	Bos'n's Mate 2d Class	San Diego, CA
Russell M. Davenport	Seaman 1st Class	Sterling Heights, MI
Albert L. Ellis	Seaman 1st Class	Hemet, CA
John W. Gercevic	Quartermaster 3d Class	Akron, OH
*Everett G. Gunning	Seaman 2d Class	Enid, OK
Harold E. Johnson	Seaman 2d Class	Oak Harbor, WA
*Stanton E. Jones	Seaman 1st Class	McAlester, OK
*Robert J. Lewis	Seaman 2d Class	Oak Forest, IL
Clayton W. McQuay	Turret Capt. 1st Class	Huntsville, AL
Jack V. Miller	Seaman 1st Class	Clinton, OH
Clarence J. Mullaley	Seaman 1st Class	San Antonio, TX
Rufus F. Nance	Bos'n's Mate 2d Class	Hayward, CA
Westley F. Potts	Bos'n's Mate 2d Class	Mancos, CO
Howard E. Roberts, Jr.	Coxswain	San Diego, CA
Herbert Fox Rommel	Ensign	Newport, RI
**Albert F. Sandall	Coxswain	Galesburg, IL
Michael J. Savarese	Seaman 1st Class	Lake Grove, NY
William P. Schauf	Seaman 2d Class	Albany, NY
Frank H. Scott	Seaman 1st Class	Sioux City, IA
James E. Stallings	Seaman 2d Class	Winter Garden, FL
Louis C. Templeton	Bos'n's Mate 1st Class	El Cajon, CA
Richard F. Whitman	Gunner's Mate 2d Class	White Bear Lake, MN
*Norman E. Wiley	Seaman 1st Class	Flatwoods, KY

I have referred to various official documents and certain reports in the interest of accuracy.

Among these were Vice Admiral Homer N. Wallin's account of the Pearl Harbor salvage effort; the action reports of Lieutenant Commander

*Deceased
**Received the Bronze Star at Iwo Jima in 1944.

W. M. Hobby, Jr., first lieutenant in *Oklahoma;* as well as action and damage reports of Captain H. D. Bode, commanding officer, and Commander J. L. Kenworthy, Jr., executive officer, *Oklahoma.*

Official documents consulted include Rescue and Salvage Work, USS *Oklahoma* (12 December 1941), and History of USS *Oklahoma* (BB-37). Statements and recollections from survivors and other personnel from newspaper and magazine accounts and other official publications were also used. The roster list of turret no. 4—survivors and deceased—as of 8 December 1941 was furnished by Captain H. F. Rommel.

For historical accuracy and background information my two most important secondary sources were Walter Lord, *The Day of Infamy* (Holt, Rinehart, & Winston; New York, 1957) and Samuel Eliot Morison, *History of United States Naval Operations in World War II,* vol. 3, *The Rising Sun in the Pacific, 1931–April 1942* (Boston: Little, Brown, 1948).

Also helpful for details of naval life were *The Bluejackets' Manual* (1940), *Seamanship* (Navpers 16118, June 1944), and "Medal of Honor" (U.S. Government Printing Office, 1968).

Index

About the Author

Stephen Bower Young served as a seaman and petty officer in the regular navy and as a commissioned officer in the naval reserve, from which he is retired. He was awarded the Purple Heart for injuries received 7 December 1941 and a Navy Unit Commendation and five battle stars while serving in the light cruiser *Honolulu* in the Guadalcanal, New Georgia, and Aleutian campaigns during World War II. He was recalled to active duty during the Korean War and served in the attack transport *Monrovia*.

Young, a Massachusetts native, is a graduate of Harvard College, where he was commissioned from the navy's V-12 ROTC program. Retired from business, he makes his home in Boston and is currently engaged in researching his next book.

The **Naval Institute Press** is the book-publishing arm of the U.S. Naval Institute, a private, nonprofit professional society for members of the sea services and civilians who share an interest in naval and maritime affairs. Established in 1873 at the U.S. Naval Academy in Annapolis, Maryland, where its offices remain today, the Naval Institute has more than 100,000 members worldwide.

Members of the Naval Institute receive the influential monthly magazine *Proceedings* and discounts on fine nautical prints, ship and aircraft photos, and subscriptions to the quarterly *Naval History* magazine. They also have access to the transcripts of the Institute's Oral History Program and get discounted admission to any of the Institute-sponsored seminars regularly offered around the country.

The Naval Institute's book-publishing program, begun in 1898 with basic guides to naval practices, has broadened its scope in recent years to include books of more general interest. Now the Naval Institute Press publishes more than sixty new titles each year, ranging from how-to books on boating and navigation to battle histories, biographies, ship and aircraft guides, and novels. Institute members receive discounts on the Press's nearly 400 books in print.

Full-time students are eligible for special half-price membership rates. Life memberships are also available.

For a free catalog describing the Naval Institute Press books currently available, and for further information about U.S. Naval Institute membership, please write to:

Membership & Communications Department
U.S. Naval Institute
118 Maryland Avenue
Annapolis, Maryland 21402-5035
Or call, toll-free, (800) 233-8764.

THE NAVAL INSTITUTE PRESS

TRAPPED AT PEARL HARBOR
Escape From Battleship *Oklahoma*

Designed by Karen L. White

Set in Berkeley Oldstyle and Cochin
by Brushwood Graphics, Inc.
Baltimore, Maryland

Printed on 60-lb. Sebago Eggshell and 70-lb. Glatco Gloss
and bound in Holliston Roxite B vellum
by The Maple-Vail Book Manufacturing Group
York, Pennsylvania